# FIRST PEOPLE

THE EASTERN KULIN OF MELBOURNE, PORT PHILLIP & CENTRAL VICTORIA

# FIRST PEOPLE

## THE EASTERN KULIN OF MELBOURNE, PORT PHILLIP & CENTRAL VICTORIA

GARY PRESLAND

Museum Victoria Publishing

Published by Museum Victoria Publishing 2010
Reprinted 2017


Museum Victoria Publishing
GPO Box 666
Melbourne
Victoria 3001
Australia
Tel +61 3 8341 7536/7370
Fax + 61 3 8341 7573
publications@museum.vic.gov.au

www.museumvictoria.com.au
Tel +61 3 8341 7777

Design by Elizabeth Dias,
MV Studios Museum Victoria
Typeset by Prowling Tiger Press
Printed in Hong Kong by The Australian Book Connection

National Library of Australia Cataloguing-in-Publication data:
Author: Presland, Gary.
Title: First people : the Eastern Kulin of Melbourne, Port Phillip and Central Victoria / Gary Presland.
ISBN: 9780980619072 (pbk.)
Notes: Includes bibliographical references and index.
Subjects: Aboriginal Australians-Victoria--Port Phillip Region--Social life and customs.
Aboriginal Australians--Victoria--Melbourne--Social life and customs.
Aboriginal Australians--Victoria--History

Dewey Number: 994.50049915

**COVER IMAGE** Body decorations of the kind seen here on these young Koorie men probably indicated clan or language group affiliation. Such markings were applied with kaolin clay and ochre.

Dr Gary Presland studied history at La Trobe University and archaeology at University of London. For the past forty years his major research interests have been in the Aboriginal history and natural history of the Melbourne area.

Gary is a Fellow of the Royal Historical Society of Victoria, an Honorary Fellow at The University of Melbourne and an Honorary Associate of Museum Victoria, where he was the 2001 Thomas Ramsay Science and Humanities Fellow.

His previous books include *The Place for a Village*, which won the 2009 Victorian Community History Award for Best Book, and *For God's sake send the trackers.*

Gary lives within the estate of the Wurundjeri-balluk.

This book is dedicated to the memory of Diane E. Barwick (1938–1986)

I AM DERRIMUT

*I am Derrimut; of lore and ancient knowledge have I sung*
*Of a time before the Ngamajet stole our being*
*In misty lands, where flows the Birrarung.*

*My people are Yalukit, our language Boon urrung*
*Land and people undivided, always interweaving*
*I am Derrimut; of lore and ancient knowledge have I sung.*

*We are Kulin, by kin and thought and tongue*
*Watched by Bunjil and by Waa; spirits overseeing*
*In misty lands, where flows the Birrarung.*

*The world was ever so; in the Dreaming all begun*
*Ancestral beings moved, their benevolence revealing*
*I am Derrimut; of lore and ancient knowledge have I sung.*

*I am Derrimut, Arweet of Boon urrung*
*We cared for land: by which we drew all meaning*
*In misty lands, where flows the Birrarung.*

*This land, once mine to spend my days among*
*Tho' now misnamed, its spirit yet unfleeing*
*I am Derrimut; of lore and ancient knowledge have I sung*
*In misty lands, where flows the Birrarung.*

GARY PRESLAND

# Acknowledgements

In the twenty-five years since the first edition of this book I have added to and refined my knowledge and understanding of the subject. In this I have been significantly assisted by untold numbers of people, through conversations, written and verbal, by being asked to explain myself during public talks, and through the ever increasing body of published work on all aspects of Koorie history.

In the past quarter of a century our views on Koorie culture and history have changed enormously, and are continuing to change as more and more research is carried out. Probably the most significant shift has been in the hugely increased involvement of Koorie individuals and organisations, at all levels and in all organisations and institutions of research in the area. Today a book of this kind cannot be written without Koorie participation in some way.

I am thus particularly grateful to Darren Griffen and the Wurundjeri Tribe Land and Compensation Cultural Heritage Council Inc., and to Kim Monoghan, Executive Officer, Taungurung Clans Aboriginal Corporation for providing authority to access information in the Aboriginal Heritage Register, for their respective areas. I also thank Emma Rae and Liz Kilpatrick for advice and assistance in accessing the Register.

In the preparation of this work I have also benefitted from help provided by Dr Ian D Clark, University of Ballarat; staff at the State Library of Victoria, particularly in Picture Collections; and John Kean, Museum Victoria, and it is a pleasure to thank them here.

My connection to Patty Brown of Museum Victoria Publishing goes back to the very beginning of this book's history. It was at her prompting that I agreed to revise and update that book, and she was instrumental in seeing the project completed. Patty also drew in Melanie Ostell as editor. For all of this I owe her a particular debt.

Finally, I am, as ever, grateful for the support of my wife, Helen Harris OAM and daughter, Penny.

# Contents

PART ONE

# PLACE, PEOPLE AND CONNECTIONS

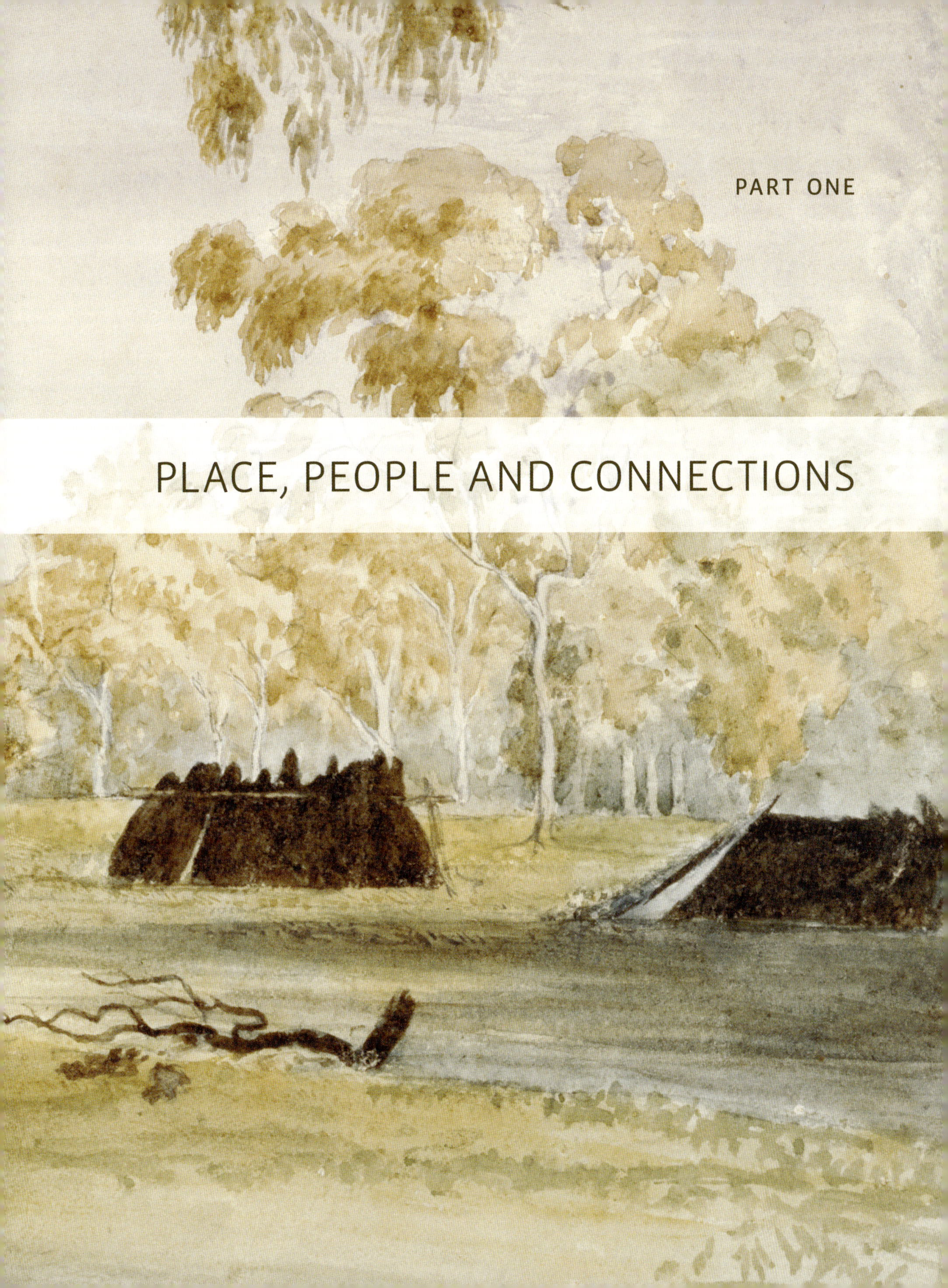

CHAPTER ONE

# The Kulin Landscape

The landscapes of the Eastern Kulin can be considered in two parts: those to the north of the Great Dividing Range, and those to the south. The most important connection for any individual of any clan was his or her attachment, through their place of birth, to land. Members of each clan identified with a particular tract of land; this was a connection that defined the individual's place in the world. These clan estates also provided most of the material needs of the people, on a seasonal basis. What did not occur naturally within the home range could be gathered elsewhere in the Eastern Kulin area or acquired by exchange from distant groups.

**Previous & Left**
Depictions of Koorie camps such as this by John Cotton owe something to artistic licence and convention. The posed figure with attendant dog in the foreground, and an array of shelters of different construction in the background is complemented by an overarching dome of vegetation.

## North of the range

On the northern side of the Great Dividing Range, the area of the Eastern Kulin stretched in the north–south axis from the Murray River at Echuca to the peaks of the Range. In the east–west direction the area claimed collectively by the Ngurai-illam-wurrung and Taung wurrung- speaking clans took in the drainage basins of the Campaspe, Goulburn, and Broken rivers and the upper section of Broken Creek.

About one third of the language groups' territory spread across the northern district plains, between the Murray River valley and the foothills of the Great Dividing Range, but a much larger portion of Eastern Kulin territory consisted of land within the Central Highlands, both east and west. Each of these physiographic areas was derived from a different landscape-forming process; to that extent they also presented a different range of resources for use by Eastern Kulin people.

The plains of the northern district extend from the foothills of the central highlands past Shepparton and Kyabram to the Murray River. These plains are alluvial in origin, being composed of water-borne silts of various grain size carried by the Loddon, Campaspe and Goulburn rivers during the Quaternary period, that is, within the past 2.6 million years.

The eastern and western divisions of the highlands are separated by a low gap near Kilmore, which marks a change in the elevation of the highlands. The central highlands was formed through episodes of upwarping and faulting that began in the Mesozoic era (between 225 and 65 million years ago). However, the eastern highlands are, on average, more elevated than the Western, with a number of peaks, such as Mount Buller, rising to more than 1800 metres. In contrast, in those parts of the western highlands that comprise land of the Eastern Kulin (between Lancefield and Beaufort), only Mount Macedon is more than 900 metres in height.

The geology of the highlands consists of a wide variety of rock formations that date from most geological periods. Within the territory of the Taung wurrung, a band of granitic rocks and lava flows from the Palaeozoic age (about 250 million years) forms the northern edge of the eastern highlands. The area from near Mansfield to Mount Timbertop and stretching away to the north-east, past Broken River, is underlain by sandstones and conglomerate laid down during the Devonian period (about 380 million years ago). However, the greater part of this end of the eastern highlands, stretching south to the dividing line between river catchments north and south of the ranges, comprises sedimentary and metamorphic rocks of even greater age. These extensive sediments date from the Silurian period (about 440 million years ago) and stretch as far as the Yarra River to make up the larger part of the eastern side of the Port Phillip landscape. It is in the area of these Silurian sandstones that Aboriginal craftsmen obtain the fine-grained cherts and silcretes that they use to make the best stone points, blades and scrapers.

In a couple of areas, such as near the Howqua River and in the region between Lancefield and Heathcote, metamorphic greenstone outcrops at the surface. These narrow belts occur along major fault axes, principally on the northern side of the Great Dividing Range. This greenstone is from the Cambrian period, and at more than 500 million years of age it is the oldest geological material in Victoria. These outcrops were of great importance to the Eastern Kulin because this hard rock was particularly favoured as material for making hatchet heads; in fact the greenstone from Mount William was the central commodity in a trading network that stretched hundreds of kilometres from the source.

On the alluvial plains between the Murray River and the foothills of the highlands, the predominant vegetation regime was grassland, with areas of grassy woodlands where the elevations began to increase. The grasslands supported a rich diversity of species, including Kangaroo Grass, Wallaby Grass and Common Tussock-grass. The plains woodlands supported a larger number of mature plants, such as trees and shrubs; where the land was higher the woodlands gave way to forests, reflecting greater rainfall.

The northern side of the highlands, below the lower slopes and above the alluvial plain of the Murray River, was dominated by Box-Ironbark woodlands. On the low hills, generally between 150 and 300 metres in altitude, plant communities were dominated by Grey Box and Red Box, Yellow Gum (White Ironbark) and Red Ironbark. The understorey varied according to geographic location but often included Cherry Ballart and small-leafed acacias such as Gold-dust Wattle; heaths and shrubby daises were often present also.

## South of the range

On the southern side of the range, in the land of the Woi wurrung, Boon wurrung and Watha wurrung, there was a diversity of geological forms. The city of Melbourne today spreads across five different geological bases, each of which has been shaped over aeons of time to create the landscape we see today. It is easy to observe a marked increase in elevation as one moves from the flat plains on the western side of Port Phillip Bay, across the heavily weathered Silurian surface of the eastern side of the bay to the Dandenong Ranges. This variation in height above sea level is a result of the geological history of the area and major contributing factor to the differences in the weather and hydrology across the area.

The Yarra River, the defining natural history feature of the area runs through this landscape. Some parts of the river are one hundred million years old while in other stretches the river runs over landforms that were formed less than 800,000 years ago. In many places, from the higher country in the east to its mouth at the top of Port Phillip Bay, the course of the river forms a dividing line between the different geological formations of this region. Most of the Yarra's tributary streams, including the major one, the Maribyrnong, flow from the north, an indication of the slight slope to the south that is a feature of the land between the Great Dividing Range and the southern edge of the continent.

The oldest geological formation in the region, the bedrock of Melbourne, is the series of Silurian-aged deposits that comprise the elevated parts of the eastern side of metropolitan area. This is the same formation that makes up the surface of the eastern Highlands in their westernmost extension. These 440-million-year-old sand- and mudstone sediments underlie the greater part of Melbourne's eastern suburbs, from the eastern side of the Central Business District to the foothills of the Dandenongs, broken in only a few places by more recent formations.

The Dandenong Ranges themselves were formed during the Devonian period, following the folding and faulting of the Silurian layers. Mount Dandenong is, at 633 metres, the highest point in the Port Phillip region, and was formed when acid volcanics were extruded into a cauldron collapse area created by adjacent faults in the rock. In four phases, rhyolites and dacite flowed out at the surface and created the ranges. Its southern reaches around Lysterfield and Berwick are also the result of volcanic action during the Devonian period, but in this case the igneous material—granites and granodiorites—was intruded *under* the surface. This occurred when the material was forced up through the surrounding rock, probably through fault lines that had developed during the earlier folding and faulting.

The land surface to the south of the Silurian sediments, stretching away from the Yarra to take in all of the south-eastern suburbs of Melbourne, is also sedimentary in nature but of a much younger age. These sandstones date from the Tertiary period and are only about three to four million years old.

Within the same geological time frame, but preceding the later deposition phases of these sediments, there was also volcanic activity in the Port Phillip region about forty-two and fifty-seven million years ago. The lava that was extruded through the overlying rock at that time today forms the western side of the CBD, from Elizabeth Street to Spencer Street. The most prominent feature of this formation, Batman's Hill, is at the southern extent of a ridge of this volcanic material. The ridge of olivine basalt stretches to the north-east and takes in Flagstaff Hill, Hotham Hill and some of the higher parts of Essendon. The small conical hill directly south of the Yarra River valley (called Emerald Hill by the European settlers because of its coverage of lush green vegetation) owes much of its shape to this volcanic activity, although it is capped by the later Tertiary sediments. This volcanic formation is referred to as the 'older volcanics' to distinguish it from more recent volcanic activity.

'Newer volcanics' began about 4.5 million years ago and continued to about 820,000 years ago. Within that period there was a number of separate eruptions and outpourings of lava from volcanoes to the north of Port Phillip Bay: between the Sunbury/Gisborne area and the Great Dividing Range, there are at least twelve eruption points, all of which were active in the past five million years. A large part of the northern area of Melbourne also sits on a basalt plain, created during this same phase of volcanism. In the period between 1.06 and 0.82 million years ago, an enormous volume of fluid basalt streamed out of Mount Fraser, near Beveridge, more than 40 km to the north of the bay. This molten rock flowed to the south, filling the ancient valleys of the Darebin and Merri creeks. Lapping around the higher points of Silurian and

Carrum Swamp was once the largest wetland in the Port Phillip region, and a major source of materials and food for Boon wurrung and clans. Its original extent can be appreciated when plotted against contemporary street maps.

Tertiary sediments, the lava blanketed the lower-lying areas between Darebin Creek and Moonee Ponds Creek, and reached as far to the south as the Yarra River at Richmond.

In a number of places around the territories of the Woi wurrung and Boon wurrung the topography is a result of comparatively recent deposits of silts and sands. Deposits of these types occurred within the epoch called Holocene (within the last ten thousand years) and comprise the valleys and river flats around the major streams of the area. These sediments are either alluvial (river-borne) or colluvial (consisting of detrital material moved essentially by gravity) and in the lower stretches of the Yarra River valley they have a depth of about 30 metres. Over thousands of years accumulated sediment also raised the low-lying areas of South Melbourne and St Kilda to their present level. The two largest and most significant areas of Holocene-aged deposits in this region are the combined estuary of the Yarra and Maribyrnong rivers at the top of Port Phillip Bay, and Carrum Swamp, a wetland of about 30 square kilometres on the eastern side of the bay.

The vegetation across the Port Phillip region varies according to the geology and rainfall. On the western basalt plains, tussock grasses such as Kangaroo Grass (*Themeda triandra*) dominated, with trees such as Sheoak (*Allocasaurina* sp.) only growing along major streams. Open woodlands dominated by River Red Gum (*Eucalyptus camaldulensis*) and Yellow Box (*E. melliodora*) covered large areas on the northern side of the Yarra river and the more elevated areas to the east were clothed in forests, ranging in type from relatively open Valley Heathy Forest in the Box Hill area to denser forests of Long-leaved Box (*E. Goniocalyx*) and various stringybark species further to the east.

## Watha wurrung territory

Some of the geomorphological processes that shaped the landscapes surrounding Port Phillip Bay also affected the Bellarine Peninsula and adjacent areas, the territory of Watha wurrung clans. The only surface features within these clan estates that date from before the Tertiary period are the higher parts—the Barrabool Hills, You Yangs and Brisbane Ranges. At Dog Rocks, and in a couple of places within the Barrabool Hills there are outcrops of Cambrian diorite. This rock is similar to the material sourced at Mount Howqua and Mount William and as with those sites, these places were of particular economic value to local clans.

## People in the landscape

Aboriginal people had been living on the land of the Eastern Kulin for perhaps up to 40,000 years before Europeans arrived. Aborigines themselves arrived in this part of Australia before the last Ice Age began. Through 1600 generations they adapted to the varying climatic conditions and the resultant changes in the nature and extent of their territories. Over that long stretch of time, as with all human groups, the way they lived and interacted with the land also brought changes to their surroundings.

The landscape features of Eastern Kulin territory—the hills, valleys and plains, the course of the rivers, the shape of the bay itself—have formed over millions of years. Some of these features, such as the size of the bay, the ground surface of some inner Melbourne suburbs, and the vegetation cover, were formed within the past ten thousand years. In the case of local vegetation patterns, Aboriginal resource management practice played a significant role in the changes that occurred in this period.

The natural processes that created these landscapes, however, were slow and gradual: it took more than 3,000 years for the water level in the bay to drop one metre. The landscapes of the region are still being reshaped at much the same pace, through natural agencies of change. We tend not to notice the work of these processes, partly because of their slow speed, and partly because there is another, more rapid cause of change in play: human action. Since the arrival of European settlers, changes to the landscape have been rapid and vast, particularly in the area around Port Phillip Bay. Batman's Hill has been completely removed, the course of the Yarra River has changed extensively and is now about two kilometres shorter. Large areas of wetland which were close to the city have since been drained.

Indeed, nowhere in the land of the Eastern Kulin are the landscapes unchanged from those first encountered by Europeans in the nineteenth century. The impact of the presence of Europeans has been to alter massively the environments that were an integral part of an ancient way of life. These environments were certainly the physical means of support for Aboriginal people, but they were much more than that. In Aboriginal society, the land and people were a unified whole. Although Europeans had no sense of it, in occupying the land to the exclusion of its former owners they were in essence destroying the culture of those people directly.

[illegible]
& his Lubra

No 2 Billibellary Chief of Yar[illegible]
[T]ribe on Settlement being formed

CHAPTER TWO

# The People

On 28 March 1839, when European settlement in Victoria was less than five years old, between four and five hundred Koories congregated in a camp in the area which is now the Royal Botanic Gardens. These people had come to form a welcoming party for the newly arrived Chief Protector of Aborigines, George Augustus Robinson. In the days before this event, Robinson's Assistants had gathered Koories from all around the district into the settlement, perhaps even as far as the Murray River, near Echuca. Not all were from the same clan or language group, though these groups were certainly connected. There were, in fact, up to four separate language groups from around the Port Phillip District of New South Wales.

At the time Europeans first settled south of the Murray River, in what is now called Victoria, there were hundreds of Aboriginal clans living in the area. These clans were grouped according to the languages their members spoke. The settlement on the Yarra River, established by Europeans in 1835, was within the clan estates of two separate groups. These groups were referred to by white people as tribes, although the term used today is 'language group'.

Billibellary, the clan-head of one of the Wurundjeri-willam patrilines of Woi wurrung speaker. In the 1840s he was one of the most influential clan-heads of the Eastern Kulin, and one of the custodians of the Mount William stone quarry.

The two language groups in the Melbourne area—called Woi wurrung and Boon wurrung—spoke closely related languages and collectively claimed the area south of the Great Dividing Range, from the Werribee River to the height of the Dandenong Ranges. The similarities of their languages with those of a number of other groups within the regions of central and western Victoria, connected the Woi wurrung and Boon wurrung to a confederacy or nation called 'Kulin'. These two language groups, along with the Taung wurrung and Ngurai-illum wurrung (whose territories were on the northern side of the Great Dividing Range), made up what is now referred to as the Eastern Kulin. The eponymous term 'Kulin' was used in all these groups to refer to human beings. Anybody who was not a member of a Kulin clan was considered a different sort of human being.

There was a high degree of similarity in the languages spoken by the clans of the Eastern Kulin. Indeed, they had such a high percentage of words in common that some linguists have suggested there was only one Eastern Kulin language, with a north and south regional variation. Recent studies indicate that speakers of Woi wurrung, in the area drained by the Yarra River, and Boon wurrung, who claimed all of the Mornington Peninsula, had as much as 93 per cent of their vocabularies in common. Woi wurrung and Taung wurrung speakers, from the Goulburn and Broken River basins, had 83 per cent in common, and those clans speaking Boon wurrung and Taung wurrung had 80 per cent in common. In the north of the Eastern Kulin territory, Ngurai-illum wurrung clans, in the area between Echuca and Murchison, spoke the Taung wurrung language. In part, the closeness of the Eastern Kulin languages is indicated by the similarity of their names: the common suffix '(w)urrung' can be understood as 'mouth/lips', meaning language. The prefix in the name, that is Woi or Boon, is the way in which the negative is expressed in that language.

The commonality of these Eastern Kulin languages distinguished their speakers from clans who spoke other Kulin languages—members of the Western Kulin and the Watha wurrung. There were eight Western Kulin languages, spoken by clans in an area from the Murray River to the Wimmera and Mallee and east almost to the Campaspe River. Western Kulin

Mr King, a clan-head of one of the Taung wurrung clans.

languages shared only about 40 per cent common vocabulary with Eastern Kulin languages. Watha wurrung was a separate Kulin language, and had almost 50 per cent common vocabulary with Eastern Kulin. This language was spoken by clans whose estates took in the Bellarine Peninsula, as well as an area that included Ballarat and Beaufort and stretched as far to the west as Fiery Creek.

Although language was a major element linking members of the Eastern Kulin confederacy, these clans also shared a number of other social factors.

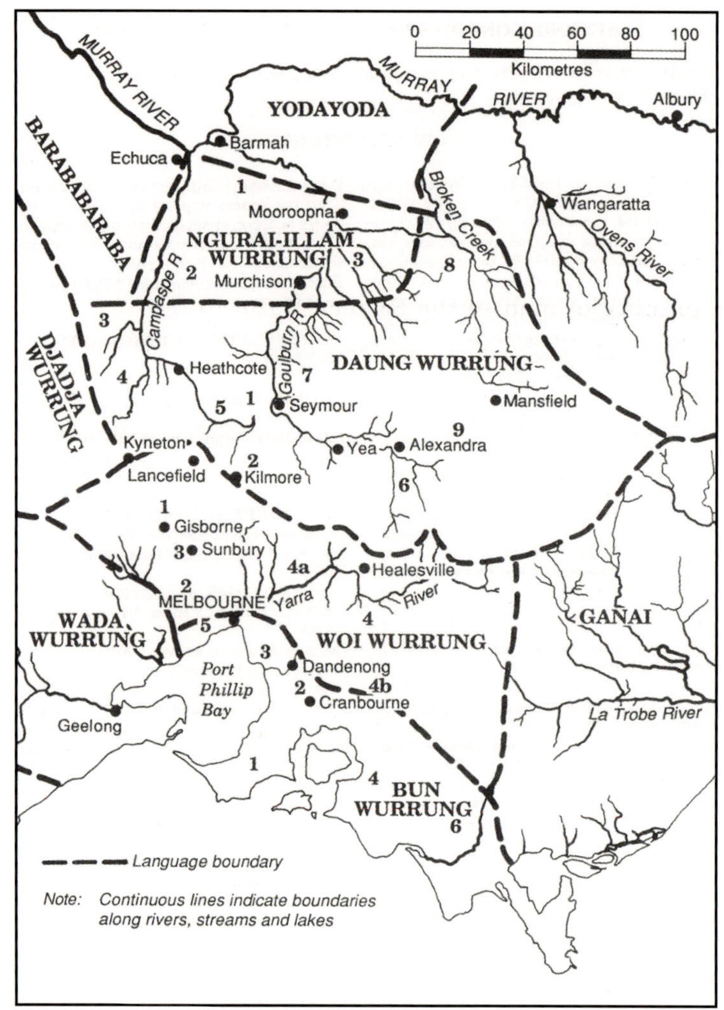


Eastern Kulin language areas and clans. For key to numbering, see Tables on pages 24, 25, 26, 27. The historical record contains many alternative renderings of language group names; researchers have added more. These maps, along with the names, come from the work of Ian Clark.

They shared, for example, common beliefs regarding Dreaming figures. All Kulin members believed the world was created by Bunjil and Waa, and a range of lesser spirit ancestors. Bunjil (who took the shape of an eaglehawk), and Waa (a crow), were the major ancestors who created both humans and the Aboriginal world during the Dreaming. The Kulin clans believed that the living world was divided into two halves, also named Bunjil and Waa after the major creator spirits.

It was the practice of men in the Eastern Kulin to seek marriage partners from within the confederacy but outside of their own clan. Indeed, this practice may have provided one of the bases of their confederacy. It appears that some groups were more likely than others to exchange women as brides. The Boon wurrung and Watha wurrung clans had such a connection and were also connected by ceremonial bonds. Although Watha wurrung was not an Eastern Kulin language, members of this language group were connected to the Eastern Kulin in a variety of other ways. With Eastern Kulin, Watha wurrung formed a cultural bloc and its members were linked by kin and thought and tongue.

There were two language groups within the broader Kulin confederacy whose territories bordered Port Phillip Bay. On the western side of the bay the estates of the Watha wurrung-speaking clans took in the Bellarine Peninsula and stretched to the north and west around the northern side of the Otway Ranges. Their eastern range went as far as the Werribee River. On the eastern side of Port Phillip Bay, Boon wurrung-speaking clans claimed the Mornington Peninsula, the southern reaches of the Dandenongs, the area around Westernport Bay, and as far to the east as Wilsons Promontory. One of the Boon wurrung clans, the Yalukit willam identified with a corridor of land that stretched from St Kilda, on the southern side of the Yarra, to the eastern side of the Werribee River.

The clans of the Woi wurrung language group collectively claimed all of the area drained by the Yarra River and its tributaries, and shared borders with both these language groups.

The remaining two language groups making up the Eastern Kulin were the Taung wurrung and the Ngurai-illum wurrung. The land of the

Taung wurrung stretched north from the Great Dividing Range and included the upper parts of the Campaspe and Goulburn rivers and Broken Creek. Bordering this group's northern land, and taking in the downstream courses of the Campaspe and Goulburn rivers, was the territory of the Ngurai-illum wurrung.

The boundaries of these language group territories were likely indicated by landscape features. The dividing line between Woi wurrung and Boon wurrung, for example, was aligned on a drainage basin; where water drained into the Yarra River it was within Woi wurrung territory, where it flowed into the Bay or into Bass Strait it was Boon wurrung. These boundaries were well known to members of the different groups and never lightly crossed; any resources that occurred within a clan's estate were available for use by that clan, but people from a different clan needed permission to enter the estate and make use of it.

It would be a mistake, however, to think of these boundaries as fixed. In the traditional situation there may well have been some flexibility as to their location; they were boundaries intimately known to all the people concerned, but that might vary from time to time. Lines drawn on maps that represent clan or language group boundaries as seen by European observers should be regarded as approximate; they only reflect the situation at the time of first contact between Koories and Europeans, without any surety that earlier times are also reflected. Language group boundaries were really social in nature and cannot be accurately rendered on paper.

There was another large group like the Eastern Kulin who lived to their east, in Gippsland. These people called themselves Kurnai or Gunai and spoke a completely different language from that of the Kulin clans. At the time of European settlement, Kulin and Kurnai were on unfriendly terms and only met to fight when one group invaded the territory of the other. Archaeological evidence also indicates that there was no trade between the two groups. A particular type of stone for making hatchet heads, which comes from Mount William and was widely traded through Kulin territory and beyond, has been found only rarely in Kurnai territory.

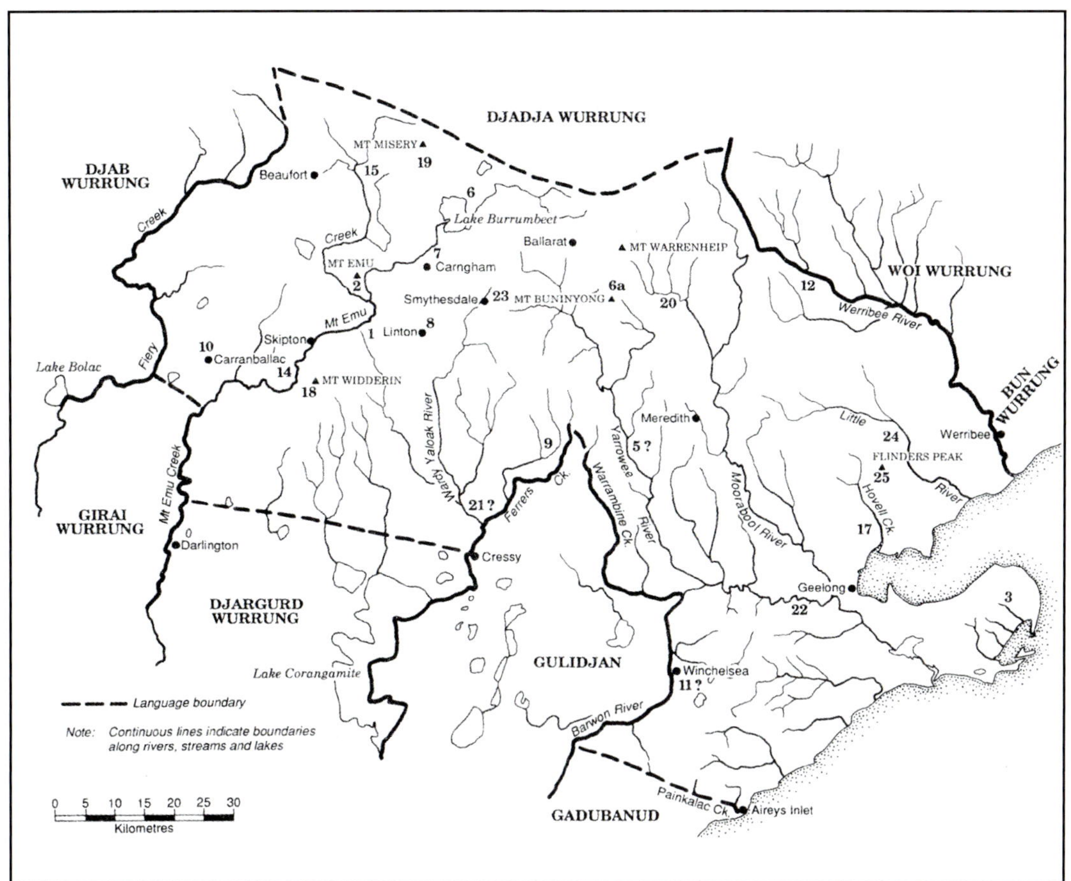


Watha wurrung language area and clans. For key to numbering, see Tables on pages 28, 29. Note the alternative spelling of the language group name, as used by Ian Clark.

## Koorie society

As with all human societies, traditional Koorie society operated at a number of different levels. Language groups such as the Taung wurrung comprised numerous smaller groups, each of which was arranged around a particular organising principle. The most important social group within Koorie society was the clan because it was the land-owning unit. It was also the group with which an individual Koorie would identify herself or himself. All individuals born into a given clan spoke the same language and identified with a particular area of land, or estate, which they regarded as their own since the time of the Dreaming or creation. Clan's might be considered as a very large extended family, since everybody born into the clan shared a common ancestor.

Each Kulin clan was essentially independent, and governed by collective decisions. In each clan there were one or two clan-heads, individuals whose role it was to put their clan's position at the council meetings of clan-heads, which was the nearest thing in Koorie society to a governing body. At the time of European settlement on Kulin land Billibellary, the clan-head of the Wurundjeri willam patriline of Woi wurrung, was considered the pre-eminent Kulin clan-head, whose voice carried extra weight. Within their clan, clan-heads such as Billibellary provided guidance and advice during group discussion and carried the decisions to council meetings. Their standing within the clan might have allowed them to exercise control of marriages but otherwise clan-heads had no special privileges.

In the Woi wurrung and Taung wurrung clans these positions were called Ngurungaeta; in the Boon wurrung clans they were Arweet. In each Kulin clan these titles were neither automatically inherited nor elected. Often, a clan-head, towards the end of his life, would nominate his successor, but that person had both to prove his competence and win the endorsement of clan-heads from other Kulin clans.

This sketch of Nerenunnin throwing a tirrer with a wongim in his left hand is an interesting indication of the basic toolkit carried by men. In addition to the spear (*tirrer*) and spearthrower (*wongim*), Nerenunnin also has a hatchet tucked in his waist belt.

A single clan could number in the hundreds, which was too large a group to be practical for most day-to-day purposes. For daily economic functioning, clan members operated in smaller family-based units, often referred to as bands. These bands would comprise fifteen to twenty

Nerenunnin Throwing a Tirrer

individuals, generally of one or two families, plus visitors. Although sometimes widely dispersed in such groups, members of a clan would know where their fellow clanspeople were. Clan members might also, by arrangement, temporarily join a band operating within the area of a different language group of the Eastern Kulin. Reasons for doing this include taking advantage of seasonal abundances in food, meeting with other members of a totemic group and fulfilling ritual obligations, or visiting relations.

## The Eastern Kulin clans and their estates

Precise population figures for traditional Koorie clans of the Port Phillip area are difficult to determine. The Boon wurrung clans, for example, had contact with sealers and whalers from the beginning of the nineteenth century, which affected their numbers. There is some evidence, too, that numbers declined because of a disastrous encounter with a Kurnai group from Gippsland some years prior to the beginning of European settlement. At the first official census of Kulin clans, taken in 1839, only 83 Boon wurrung were recorded, yet it may well have been the case that others were away from the settlement at the time, continuing to practice time-honoured economic and social activities.

### BOON WURRUNG CLANS

There were six clans who spoke Boon wurrung and whose estates were contiguous. Collectively these Boon wurrung clans identified with that area which now makes up the southern and south-eastern suburbs of Melbourne, taking in all the Mornington Peninsula, the catchment area of Westernport Bay and Wilsons Promontory. The eastern border of their territory was at the Tarwin River where it flows into Andersons Inlet. Boon wurrung territory also included the coastal strip around the top of Port Phillip Bay to the Werribee River. In geographic terms, they saw their territory as the area in which the streams drained to the south, or away from the Yarra.

The Boon wurrung are sometimes referred to as the 'Westernport tribe' and sometimes as the 'coast tribe'. This is likely because white people at the time thought they lived along the coast. And the Boon wurrung clans seemed to have had a closer connection with the Watha wurrung of the Bellarine Peninsula than with the other Kulin clans, which helps explain the coastal strip around the top of the bay (the estate of the Yalukit willam clan) that acted as a 'corridor' to allow easy contact between the two groups.

### WOI WURRUNG CLANS

The four Woi wurrung clans collectively claimed all that area drained by the Yarra River and its tributaries. Thus their domain was bordered in the south by Mordialloc Creek (the northern limit of the Boon wurrung), in the west by the Werribee River, in the north by the Great Dividing Range, and in the east it stretched into the Dandenong Ranges past Warburton.

Members of the Wurundjeri clans of Woi wurrung were seen around the settlement more often than those from other groups and because of this the Woi wurrung are often referred to in the historical literature as Wurundjeri. They were also called the 'Yarra Yarra tribe' and the 'Port Phillip tribe'. Other clans of Woi wurrung were also mistakenly identified as separate tribes such as the Gunung willam balluk, which were referred to as 'the Mount Macedon tribe' because they were frequently seen in that area.

### TAUNG WURRUNG CLANS

The nine Taung wurrung clans occupied the area that was drained by the Broken, Delatite, Goulburn, Coliban and Campaspe rivers, the territory being bounded on the south by the Great Dividing Range. The Tuang wurrung are referred to in the historical literature by a variety of names including the 'Devil's River tribe' and the 'Goulburn tribe'.

### NGURAI-ILLUM WURRUNG CLANS

The northern-most language group within the Eastern Kulin comprised three clans that distinguished their language with the name Ngurai-illum wurrung. There is some uncertainty today as to whether these three clans spoke a separate dialect, or (as some linguists believe) used the Taung wurrung language. These three clans occupied the lower Campaspe and Goulburn rivers between the neighbouring Taung wurrung speakers and the Murray junction.

WATHA WURRUNG CLANS

Although the Watha wurrung language had only 50 per cent common vocabulary with the Eastern Kulin languages, members of Watha wurrung-speaking clans had many other connections with the Eastern Kulin. The late Diane Barwick, a Canberra-based anthropologist, identified sixteen Watha wurrung clans in her influential 1985 study. This number was increased to twenty-six in Clark's listing of 1990 and reproduced here, although the location of some of these clans was unknown. The collective territory claimed by the Watha wurrung clans was the area west of the Werribee River and south of the Great Dividing Range, across the northern area of the Otway Ranges, as far to the west as Fiery Creek, that also encompassed the Bellarine Peninsula. The city of Geelong lies within the traditional estates of two of these clans—Watha wurung bulluk and Tooloora bulluk.

In 1803 a party of Europeans led by Lieutenant Colonel David Collins spent several months in the Sorrento area in an attempt to form a settlement. Collins found it bleak and dry and the party soon left for Van Diemen's Land, where they founded Hobart. They left behind at least one escaped convict, William Buckley, who had fled the Sorrento camp on Christmas Day 1803, with two other escapees. The three made their way around the bay, to the Swan Island area. Buckley's companions decided to return to camp but Buckley moved further to the west. After some time spent wandering around the Barwon Heads area, he was encountered by members of a local Watha wurrung clan. They took him in and he lived with the clan for the next 32 years. It was the arrival of Batman's party at Indented Head in June 1835 that attracted Buckley's interest and awakened in him a desire to re-enter European society. His published reminiscences of his thirty-two years with Watha wurrung today provide invaluable information about the pre-European way of life of Aboriginal people in the Port Phillip area.

William Buckley lived with Watha wurrung clans for 32 years, after escaping from the Sorrento settlement on Christmas Day 1803. Following European settlement he worked briefly as an interpreter and go-between, but found it difficult to re-enter European society.

W. MACLEOD

**TABLE 1**

BOON WURRUNG CLANS

| NO. | CLAN NAME | CLAN-HEAD (ARWEET) | AREA | MOEITY |
| --- | --- | --- | --- | --- |
| 1 | Burinyung bulluk | Bobinuren | Point Nepean/Cape Schanck area | Waa |
| 2 | Mayone bulluk | Budgery Tom | Carrum Swamp and inland to top of Westernport Bay; also northern area of Mornington Peninsula | Bunjil |
| 3 | Ngaruk willam | (1) Tuolwing (Ngurungaeta = the Woi wurrung term; (2) Poliorong (from late 1839) | Brighton and Mordialloc; (Barak claimed this area was 'half good', suggesting that it was open for both Woi wurrung and Boon wurrung people to use) | Bunjil |
| 4 | Yallock willam | Warendedolong | Bass River between Westernport Bay and the Dandenongs | Bunjil |
| 5 | Yalukit willam | (1) Derrimut (2) Benbow | St Kilda, Port Melbourne, south side of Yarra River to Werribee River in the west | Bunjil |
| 6 | Yowengerre | Pur.rine | Tarwin River watershed/ Wilsons Promontory | Bunjil |

**TABLE 2**

WOI WURRUNG CLANS

| NO. | CLAN NAME | CLAN-HEAD (NGURUNGAETA) | AREA | MOEITY |
|---|---|---|---|---|
| 1 | Gunung willam balluk | Ningulabul | South of Great Dividing Range around Mount Macedon and Bacchus Marsh | Bunjil |
| 2 | Kurung jang balluk | Bet Banger | Inland of Yalukit willam (Boon wurrung) in the area between Kororoit Creek and Werribee River | Waa |
| 3 | Marin balluk | Bungarim | The area between the Maribyrnong River and Kororoit Creek | Waa |
| 4A | Wurundjeri balluk (Wurundjeri willam patriline, in three sections) | (1) Billibellary | (1) Northern side of the Yarra River, from Maribyrnong River to Darebin Creek | Waa |
| | | (2) Bebejan | (2) About Heidelberg, to source of Yarra River | |
| | | (3) Bor-on-up-ton | (3) South bank of the Yarra from Gardiners Creek upstream to Yarra flats and northern slopes of the Dandenong Ranges | |
| 4B | Wurundjeri balluk (Baluk willam patriline) | Mr DeVilliers | From upper Yarra, south east to Koo-wee-rup Swamp and headwaters of LaTrobe River, southwest near to Cranbourne/ Dandenong | Waa |

**TABLE 3**

TAUNG WURRUNG CLANS

| NO. | CLAN NAME | CLAN-HEAD (NGURUNGAETA) | AREA | MOEITY |
|---|---|---|---|---|
| 1 | Buthera balluk | Cor.me.wor.rer. min | Goulburn River near Seymour | Bunjil |
| 2 | Leuk willam | Wy.er.ro.loon | Campaspe River near Kilmore | Waa |
| 3 | Moomoomgoondeet | Kerrepn.enin | West of Campaspe River | Bunjil |
| 4 | Nattarak balluk | Jille Jille | Coliban and Upper Campaspe rivers, north of Mount Martha | Waa |
| 5 | Nira balluk | Yabbee | Creeks and hills about Kilmore | Waa |
| 6 | Waring-illum balluk | Bunderboweik | Upper Goulburn River and its southern sources | Bunjil |
| 7 | Yarran-illam | Berrut | East side of Goulburn below Seymour | Bunjil |
| 8 | Yeerun-illam balluk | Baalwick | Broken River above and below Benalla | Bunjil |
| 9 | Yowung-illam balluk | Bitteruc | Alexandra and Upper Goulburn, at Mansfield | Waa |

**TABLE 4**

NGURAI-ILLAM CLANS

| NO. | CLAN NAME | CLAN-HEAD (NGURUNGAETA) | AREA | MOEITY |
|---|---|---|---|---|
| 1 | Benbedora balluk | Woer.gon.mill | Both sides of the Campaspe River at its junction with the Murray, to Elmore/Goorngong | Bunjil |
| 2 | Gunung yellam | Chimbri | Lower Campaspe, upstream of Benbedora balluk | Waa |
| 3 | Nooraialum balluk | Weeng.her.bil | Goulburn River, north of Mitchellstown, at Murchison, to within 64 km of Goulburn/Murray junction | Bunjil |

**TABLE 5**

WATHA WURRUNG CLANS

| NO. | CLAN NAME | CLAN-HEAD (NGURUNGAETA) | AREA | MOIETY |
|---|---|---|---|---|
| 1 | Barere barere bulluc | Wang.hone.beet | 'Colac' and 'Mount Bute' stations | Unknown |
| 2 | Beeriquart bulluc | William | Mount Emu | Waa |
| 3 | Bengalat bulluk | Nullaboin | Indented Head | Waa |
| 5 | Borogundidj | Not identified | Yarrowee River | Unknown |
| 6 | Borumbeet bulluk | Balybalip | Lakes Burrumbeet and Learmonth | Bunjil |
| 6A | Kureet bulluc | Morote.konung | Mount Buninyong | Bunjil |
| 7 | Coringum bulluc | Neer.mer.mulger | Carngham | Unknown |
| 8 | Carninje bulluc | Ly.je.wor.roke | 'Emu Hill' Station, Lintons Creek | Waa |
| 9 | Carrac bulluc | Teer.re.bim. mone | 'Commeralghip' station and Kuruc-a-ruc Creek | Unknown |
| 10 | Corrin corringer bulluc | Not identified | Carranbulluc | Waa |
| 11 | Gerarlture | Not identified | West of Lake Modewarre | Unknown |
| 12 | Marpeang bulluk | Worope Mr Malcolm | Blackwood, Myrniong, Bacchus Marsh | Bunjil |
| 14 | Moijerre bulluc | Pan.nong.il.jon | Mount Emu Creek | Bunjil |
| 15 | Mone bulluc | Not identified | 'Trawalla' Station, Mount Emu Creek | Waa |

| | | | | |
|---|---|---|---|---|
| 17 | Neerer bulluc | Not identified | Between Geelong and the You Yangs | Unknown |
| 18 | Pakeheneek bulluc | King Billy | Mount Widderin | Unknown |
| 19 | Peeruk-el-moom bulluk | Pikim.yowere | Near Mount Misery | Bunjil |
| 20 | Tolloora bulluk | (1) Koo.mung. ur.ruk<br>(2) Bondouin<br>(3) Karum | Mount Warrenheip. Lal Lal Creek, west branch of Moorabool River | Waa |
| 21 | Woodealoke conedeet | Not identified | Wardy Yallock River, south of Kuruc-a-ruc Creek | Unknown |
| 22 | Watha wurrung bulluc | Wolmudgin | Barrabool Hills | Bunjil |
| 23 | Wongerrer | Dang.her.ner. en.ong | Head of Woady Yallock Creek | Bunjil |
| 24 | Worinyuloke bulluk | Not identified | West side of Little River | Unknown |
| 25 | Yaawangi | Murradonnanuke | At the You Yang hills | Unknown |

CHAPTER THREE

# Interconnections in the Kulin World

What little we know of the social interconnections that existed between clans of the Eastern Kulin at the time Europeans arrived has been pieced together through the careful analysis of historical documents, as well as recent anthropological studies. The language groups within the Eastern Kulin are referred to in the surviving historical record, but there is a great deal more known about the Boon wurrung and Woi wurrung clans than other members of the Eastern Kulin. This is largely because two men who lived and worked within Boon wurrung and Woi wurrung estates over a period of years meticulously recorded their observations. George Augustus Robinson (1788–1866) was Chief Protector of Aborigines in the Port Phillip District from its formation in March 1839 until the close of the Protectorate in December 1849. During that decade he spent much of his time in contact with Koorie individuals and groups across the district, but particularly around Melbourne. He daily recorded many interactions in a journal, as well as through official reports. One of his Assistant Protectors, William Thomas (1793–1867), also lived among clans and he too made extensive notes, and wrote many reports.

William Barak's art is a distinctive blend of traditional and European elements. The subject of his work is often Aboriginal ceremony, in many cases, as here, depicting the dancers in possum skin cloaks which he drew using ochre paint. This painting also includes native fauna, emu and wallaby.

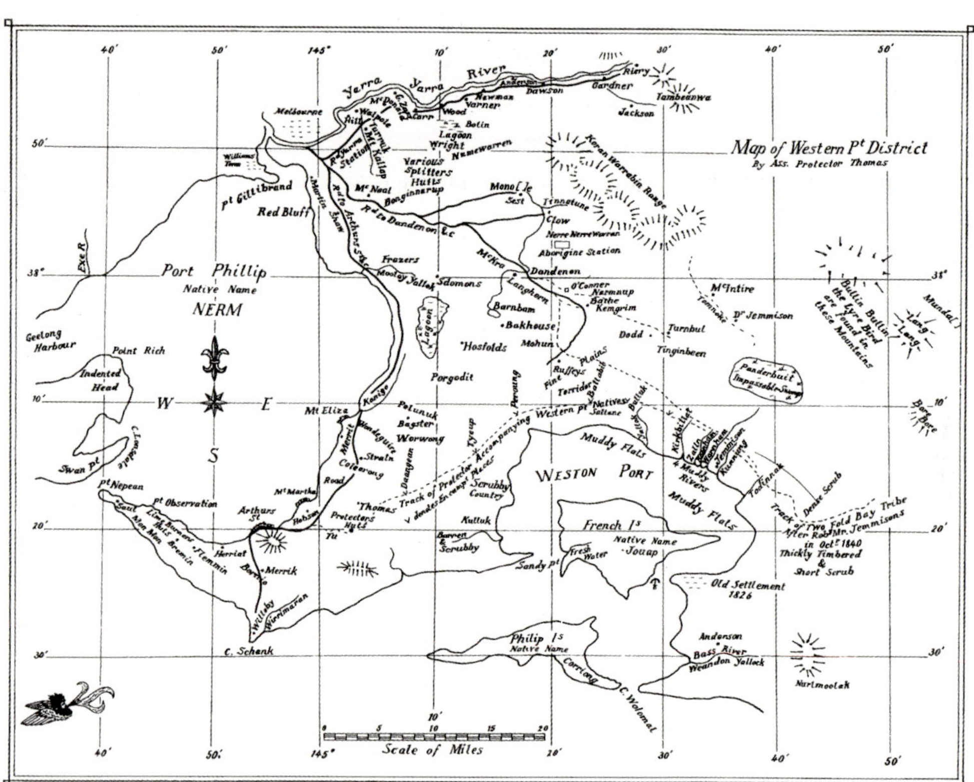

One of William Thomas's maps of the Westernport district in 1841. It shows the position of some of the early settlers, as well as the Koorie names of a number of landscape features.

These records are further supplemented by observations of Koorie activities and culture by other early European observers within the Eastern Kulin area, such as Assistant Protector James Dredge (1796–1846) and Alfred Howitt (1830–1908). It is thus possible through these historical records to gain a basic understanding of the connections and relationships that existed between clans within the Eastern Kulin nation.

As already indicated, the clans were connected in a variety of ways, such as through language, marriage and religious beliefs. Kulin clans were exogamous, that is, when a man sought a marriage partner he always looked to another clan, usually one from as far away as practical. In addition, a potential wife had to be in the opposite marriage class or 'skin-group'. For both men and women from a clan whose moeity was Bunjil, for example, marriages had to be contracted with a partner from a Waa clan; if they were Waa then they had to marry Bunjil. When young women from the Ngurai-illam-wurrung or Taung wurrung clans, north of the Great Dividing Range, reached child-bearing age they were given in marriage to men from clans south of the range. The women moved south to live with their husband in his clan. In the same way, but in the opposite direction, girls from the Woi wurrung and Boon wurrung clans moved to live with Taung wurrung husbands.

In the early 1820s, a young Ngurai-illam wurrung woman named Tooterie was given in marriage to Bebejan, a Wurundjeri willam man of the Woi wurrung language group. Bebejan was the head of his clan, a Ngurungaeta, at the time Europeans invaded Kulin territory; he was one of the eight Aboriginal men who put their mark on the Batman treaty in June 1835. Tooterie and Bebejan's son, a boy called Beruk, was also present at this meeting of John Batman, and he grew up to be the most important Kulin leader in the post-contact period. Along the way he changed his name to William Barak. Although he was born into a Woi wurrung clan, on the banks of Brushy Creek in present-day Croydon, he never ceased to be connected—through his mother's Ngurai-illam wurrung family—to the clans who lived to the north of the Great Dividing Range.

These social alliances were a way of mediating many connections between Eastern Kulin clans. These people shared a religious world view and were joined by common ceremonial practice; the family connections that joined clans also allowed individuals to travel easily for the purposes of fulfilling ritual or ceremonial obligations.

Girls were given in marriage soon after they reached child-bearing age. This union was usually arranged by the girl's father, sometimes specifically to benefit the parent. A man could increase his standing in society by aligning his family to an important man—through giving him a wife. The young girl had no influence in the matter. Moreover, for a girl coming from another clan, the first few months of married life could be difficult ones because of her lack of familiarity with local resources. If, for example, a woman from a Watha wurrung clan, who had lived most of her life in the forests of the Otway Ranges, was given in marriage to a Boon wurrung man, it's likely that she would have been unfamiliar with the sorts of foodstuffs which she would have to collect along the shore on the bay. Many men, particularly older men of standing, had more than one wife, and it was common for a young girl to be given to a man as a second or even third wife. In these situations the older wives would instruct the young girl in the ways of the clan.

There was another, ongoing advantage for the father to marry off his daughter to a man in a distant clan: a young woman given in marriage becomes more than a sexual partner and mother of her husband's children—she becomes a provider of food for the rest of her life, a feature that has interesting ramifications for on-going alliances.

In hunter–gatherer societies such as those found throughout Australia, there was a sexual division of labour—in most circumstances, men hunted and women gathered. Contrary to a long-standing misconception, it was the gathering activities of the women that provided most of the daily food supply. In accepting the gift of a wife a considerable debt is incurred by a man, which raises the issue of reciprocity. One way of repaying such a debt is to allow one's in-laws to hunt or forage in your clan's estate. Relationships of this kind existed across the entire area of the Eastern Kulin, connecting families on opposite sides of the Great Dividing Range permitting all individuals to move to a different environment when needed.

William Barak, pictured at the age of 33, was the son of Bebejan, a Woi wurrung clan-head and Tooterie, a Ngurai-illum wurrung woman. From the 1860s until his death in 1904 he was a leader of the Eastern Kulin clans, and active in the defence of the Coranderrk settlement, along with his cousin Simon Wonga.

The relationships formed by marriage alliances also affected the regular workings of totemic ritual and ceremony within the Kulin world. Aboriginal people recognised that, parallelling their physical world, there was another, spiritual realm, inhabited by the spirit beings responsible for creating the world order. These two worlds could be made to meet, through the performance of ritual at sites of special significance. Each Eastern Kulin estate had sites of this kind—places of power where the spirit beings resided in totemic form, and where members of the appropriate totemic group would gather at regular intervals.

For boys, the process of initiation into totemic groups begins when they reach the age of about ten or eleven, that is when facial hair becomes evident. Responsibility for seeing that a boy was appropriately prepared for initiation fell to the husband of the boy's sister, his brother-in-law, or to his mother's brother, his uncle. But, because of the custom of exchanging women in marriage with distant clans, these two males would have lived some distance away, and would have had to travel to the boy's clan to take part in the initiation ceremony. It is clear therefore that the bestowal of women in marriage had a bearing on the whereabouts of men within Kulin territory, as they fulfilled their ceremonial duties.

The process of initiation for men in the Kulin world took many years to complete, and men were not given a wife until they reached an appropriate level of knowledge. Since females were married at a much earlier age (although a man's first wife might be a widow) there was often still a significant age difference between men and women.

The connections that existed between Kulin clans—of both a social and spiritual nature—were maintained and strengthened at regular meetings. These gatherings were also opportunities to settle disputes and to conduct business. Such time-honoured gatherings occurred throughout the land of the Kulin. One of the places they occurred was in Woi wurrung territory, along the lower reaches of the Yarra River. As William Thomas wrote in 1840:

> *Long ere the settlement was formed, the spot where Melbourne now stands and the flat on which we are now camped [near the present-day Royal Botanic*

The patterns of scarification, referred to as cicatrices, displayed by these women were created as personal adornment. The first scars are made at puberty and more are added at intervals, into adulthood. The raised scars were created by cutting a wound and packing it with clay or ashes mixed with grease.

*Gardens] was the regular rendezvous for the (Kulin) twice a year or as often as circumstances and emergencies required to settle their grievances, revenge deaths, etc.*

On these occasions the different language groups would camp in locations determined by tradition. Thus, in the vicinity of Melbourne, Boon wurrung clans chose sites in the area of today's Botanic Gardens; the Taung wurrung traditionally camped in the vicinity of Ryrie's Hill (now Clifton Hill); and Woi wurrung were found on the site now occupied by the Melbourne Cricket Ground and Richmond Oval. Watha wurrung groups generally camped on the rising ground at the western end of Lonsdale Street.

As well as the transacting of serious business, these regular gatherings of Kulin clans were occasions for celebration. In the evenings one of the assembled clans would likely perform a corroboree. There was nothing secret or sacred about these ceremonies; the performances public displays of dancing skill and a means of conveying a new story, developed and retold by the performers. A suite of rhythm instruments including drums, clapping sticks and voice accompanied such dances. Night after night these events occurred as the clans attempted to outperform one other.

What allowed such large numbers of Koories to camp in the area was the fresh water in the Yarra River as well as the many adjacent wetlands. It was unfortunate but no coincidence that the settlement of Melbourne developed in what was a traditional meeting place for Kulin clans, the major source of fresh water in the region. In the first years of the settlement Koories still gathered in their traditional places at several locations on both sides of the Yarra. In August 1844 William Thomas noted that there was a group of Woi wurrung on the site of the Melbourne and Richmond cricket grounds, another at Newtown Hill (now Fitzroy), and the Boon wurrung were camped on a spot near where the Governor's residence now stands. It was said that when Koories from the Murray and Goulburn districts visited the settlement they camped at Ryrie's (now Clifton) Hill.

In later years, especially from the late 1840s onwards, Koories camped in parts of the settlement where there was still a remnant of the original

**Previous**
Fights between Eastern Kulin groups were not uncommon but the conflicts were generally not protracted affairs. Individuals were sometimes killed for infringements of protocol or for a perceived personal offence.

vegetation. Thus they were noted in places such as the north-west corner of Fawkner Park, in the vicinity of the Alfred Hospital and near Chapel Street, Prahran.

Although the Eastern Kulin people were united by a vast array of social connections, their relationships were not always harmonious. Disputes between groups arose from time to time and long-running feuds were not uncommon. During 1839, for example, there was a running sequence of conflicts between Woi wurrung and Watha wurrung clans, with the former group at times enlisting the help of Boon wurrung clans. In April of that year a group of 72 Watha wurrung men and women arrived in Melbourne to fight, to redress a wrong done to them by the Woi wurrung. A small group of men from Boon wurrung and Woi wurrung clans set off for a return match in August of the same year, and preparations for a third battle came in the middle of the following month. We know this because George Robinson, the Chief Protector, recorded then that Woi wurrung men were preparing spears and boomerangs to fight the Watha wurrung whom they expected in Melbourne in a matter of days. These disputes stemmed from access to resources and infringements of protocol and while such conflicts were generally short-lived, people were sometimes killed. On at least three occasions in 1839 Robinson recorded that Koories were egged on and encouraged to fight by the more rowdy white residents of Melbourne. The Protectors took a dim view of this fighting, however, physically interceding to prevent conflicts, by separating the warring parties and sometimes taking away their weapons.

It is impossible to say whether these conflicts, as recorded by Europeans, reflect a traditional picture of Koorie life or are aberrations, brought about by the presence of large numbers of whites. The main reasons for conflict in Koorie society, which include access to vital resources and the exchange of female marriage partners, were subject to a great deal of disruption from the earliest days of contact, particularly along the coast. Much of the violence witnessed by Europeans may have been a response to a rapidly changing lifestyle brought about by the sudden influx of large numbers of whites; traditional Koorie values and patterns were changing and new alliances may have been formed.

Tuat or Jack Weatherley was a Woi wurrung man who was prominent in Kulin affairs in the Western Port area and Yarra Ranges. His relationship to the Wurrundjeri clan-head Bebejan was that of brother.

PART TWO

# A WAY OF LIFE

CHAPTER FOUR

# Life on the edge of the Bay

## The hunter–gatherer way of life

As with indigenous peoples across Australia, the clans of the Eastern Kulin were hunter–gatherers. This is the oldest way of life known to the human species. Until about ten thousand years ago, when some human societies began farming, hunting and gathering had been the *only* economic and social model practiced by our species, Homo sapiens, since it first appeared in Africa about 200,000 years ago.

Scholars had long considered hunting and gathering to be a time-consuming unproductive way of fulfilling basic needs; a way of life in which people constantly chased resources. However, studies within the past fifty years on those few peoples who still practise this way of life (including some Aboriginal groups of northern and central Australia) have shown that most hunter–gatherer groups were working only about four to five hours a day. These studies were conducted on groups that live in desert environments, with far fewer resources than was the case in the relatively lush environments around Port Phillip and in central Victoria. It is likely then that Koories in this

**Previous & Left**
The Eastern Kulin fished in the many streams of their estates, using spears and nets. Nets were set in the shallows of lakes and slow streams; spears could be used from canoes, as in this idyllic scene.

Scenes such as this were often used on postcards in the first decade of the 20th century. The caption given on this 1933 card is 'Aboriginal Australian group camped in bush'.

part of Australia were working something like a thirty-hour week to satisfy their requirements for food, shelter and material supplies, and it meant that a good deal of time was available for leisure activities, maintaining tools and artefacts, and attending to spiritual and clan business.

As noted earlier, within hunter–gatherer societies there was generally a division of labour based on sex: the men hunt and the women gather. This division was borne out through observations of Eastern Kulin groups, although there were some areas of overlap, such as the preparedness of both women and children to capture small animals during their foraging activities. It was not unknown for women to hunt larger animals, but as a rule they would not if men were available to do it. While travelling with a Boon wurrung group early in 1840, William Thomas noted that while the men were away, ostensibly hunting lyrebirds in the Dandenong Ranges, the women left camp in the morning—not to gather plant foods but to go hunting.

The mistaken perception that the men were the main food suppliers in the hunter–gatherers groups may have developed because the results of their efforts, in the form of large game such as kangaroos, wallabies and emus, were more visible than the women's plants or shellfish, or much smaller animals they may have caught. A detailed study of hunter–gatherer groups around the world by Richard Lee in 1968 indicated that the relative contribution by males and females to the diet of these groups varied, in a regular fashion, according to latitude. In areas of high latitude such as the Arctic, there were far fewer gatherable resources than found in the places of low latitude such as tropics and areas of temperate clime. Among the Aboriginal groups included in Lee's study (and in those of other researchers), women consistently provided about 60 to 80 per cent of the diet.

The location of camps in the area of the Eastern Kulin was often influenced by seasonal changes. When the weather was good there was less need for shelter; base camps were established in more open locations such as along the seashore or in open river valleys. Hunting and collecting activities were focused on what was available at the given time of year so the availability of game and plant foods was a major consideration in the decision about how long a foraging group or band might stay in the one location. In most cases movement to a new site was necessary after three to four days, but in some instances, depending on the size of the group and the nature of the environment, there might be enough food for a stay of up to a week at one site.

Everything changed for the clans of the Eastern Kulin following European settlement but there is sufficient evidence, from a range of sources, to piece together an impression of what their life may have been like in different times of the year. The following account provides some idea of life in a Boon wurrung camp close to the shore of Port Phillip Bay, in the warmer months of the year.

## The Boon wurrung camp

Campsite locations were generally chosen because of the proximity of fresh water. In the regular patterns of movements by the clans around their estate, there were also favourite spots which were re-used at regular intervals. Along the edge of the bay camps were often set up in sand-dunes close to the shore, such as in the sheltered environment provided by the swale between two dune ridges running parallel to the shore. In such a location there was protection from the cool breezes off the bay in the evening while the sandy surface provided a softer place for sitting and lying than the harder ground further inland.

Camps were sometimes large, comprising a foraging band perhaps made up of several families. The size of day-to-day foraging groups could vary quite a lot; a larger camp might contain between twenty and thirty people, the number depending on factors such as the available food resources and the time of year. A group of that size would consist of perhaps four or five adult men, their wives, maybe one or two unmarried men, a couple of youths and about seven or eight children ranging in age from twelve months or less to twelve years. This was about as large as a foraging band could be and remain viable. Gatherings of larger numbers were always pre-arranged and only occurred at specific places where there were sufficient resources to sustain bigger groups. The smallest bands consisted of six or seven individuals and comprised a single family of one man, one or two wives and their children.

The depiction of fern trees in this camp scene by J S Prout might suggest an upland location for the Aboriginal camp. The composition contains sufficient of the familiar elements of Koorie material culture—spears, digging stick, baskets, fire, and a dog—to quickly convey the subject matter to the viewer.

E L M

Montefiore's hand coloured engraving of Melbourne from the falls in 1837 is based on a similar work by Robert Russell. Although the subject is said to be the township on the other side of the river, the Aboriginal camp arrangement in the foreground serves to complete the work. Note the simplicity of the lean-tos constructed as shelter. Koories frequented this area in the warmer months, so more elaborate huts were unnecessary.

The day's activities began early, usually with the rising of the sun. Fires that had been allowed to die down during the night were rekindled, breakfast was made with any leftovers from the day before and water was fetched from a nearby stream.

Over breakfast there would have been some discussion about the day's activities. The men might have gone hunting in an area less than an hour's walk inland from the camp, and along the way could spend time collecting a particular gum found in acacias such as Black Wattles (*Acacia mearnsii*). In season the gum exuded from fissures in the trunk and was collected in great quantity because it had a variety of uses. As a rare sweet foodstuff, it was a delicacy that could be eaten raw or dissolved in water. So prized was it that it was sometimes stored in quantities of up to twenty kilograms, for later use in the lean season. Gums such as this were precious, not only as sources of sugar, but also because their adhesive qualities served as a bonding agent, useful for plugging leaks in wooden water containers.

Before leaving the camp, the men collected their equipment. For hunting, they carried spears, some of which were tipped with stone points, spear throwers, a short stick or club and possibly a boomerang. Stone hatchets were taken, too, stuck in a belt made of hair or fibre. Heavier items such as the hammer-stones and nodules of stone used to make stone tools were left in camp. On occasion the men also used other specialised tools such as portable hides, which were stored in a place where they could be retrieved if needed.

The older youths, boys who had reached puberty and had begun training for manhood, went with the men. As a general rule, around eight kilometres was the maximum distance people would travel and return in one day. If a group of men needed to go further, a temporary overnight camp would be set up.

There were few animals and birds that were not hunted by the Koories. There were, however, no kangaroos within the environments close to this camp, though there were plenty of other mammal species such as the Black Wallaby, Rufous-bellied Pademelon, Echidna, Brush-tailed possum, Common Wombat, Eastern Quoll and Spot-tailed Quoll and a couple of species of Antechinus. Emus were numerous, particularly on the open plains to the south-east of the camp. These birds were speared for their meat but they also provide material for a variety of uses. Some bones from kangaroos and wallabies and emus were used as awls and bone needles in 'maintenance' activities such as making or repairing a possum-skin cloak; sinew from kangaroos and wallabies was used for binding points on spears, and for hafting wooden handles on stone hatchet heads; the skins were used for clothing and for making water bags; emu feathers were used for decoration. These materials were also used in making equipment for 'extractive' purposes such as hunting and fishing: bone was used for spear points; fur could be spun into fibre and used for making nets, carry bags and twine. 

While hunting, the men mostly relied on stealth to snare their prey, though other stratagems were sometimes employed in addition to stealth such as using a variety of hides and lures. In catching a brush turkey for example, a length of stick was prepared with a noose at one end. The man approached the turkey hidden behind a shield camouflaged with boughs and the noose was slipped over the bird's head. A similar device consisting of two sticks was used to capture hawks, where the hunter attracted the hawk with a live bird, as a lure, tied to one stick, and snared the hawk with the noose on the other stick.

After the men left camp the women would walk down to the sandy shore and spend several hours collecting shellfish from different environmental zones. By wading or diving, they collected mussels (*Mytilus sp.*), *Brachidontes*, Turbo (*Subninella*) and Limpets (*Cellana tramoserica*) from rock platforms. In the same excursion, plant foods were collected from along the shore, among which, at this time of year, was a variety of pigface which grows along coastal cliffs—the fruit of Climbing Lignum (*Muehlenbeckia adpress*), which could be ground into a flour, and Barrier Saltbush (*Enchylaena tomentose*), which had sweet berries and leaves that were eaten as a green vegetable. The main implement women had for these tasks was a wooden stick. Each woman had her own digging stick, usually with a fire-hardened point, which was used in digging roots and small animals out of burrows. They also had carry string bags, woven of twine made from the bark from Messmate (*Eucalyptus oblique*) or from rushes, as well as containers made of bark or carved from a light piece of wood.

Freshwater crayfish were one of the many resources gathered by Koories in the appropriate season, using a variety of means. In this case the method involves men wading up to their necks in water, sensing the presence of their prey with feet. One man holds a bag in his mouth, to free his hands for capturing the crayfish.

As a rule a woman who nursed did not have more than one child at the same time. While a woman was still breastfeeding a child, often until the child was three or four, she would not have another child. With only one babe in arms a woman could still collect sufficient food for herself and other members of the foraging band; with two dependent children her ability to function as a productive unit would be greatly impaired. For this reason, women would often spread the birth of children at intervals as much as four or five years. These efforts were assisted by strategies such as a postpartum sex taboo and prolonged lactation; in cases where these efforts failed, it is likely that infanticide was practised.

Children were taught by their mothers from the earliest age where they could find their own food, if necessary. For much of the time, however, they occupied themselves with games, some of which were aimed at increasing their knowledge of their surroundings.

The adult females of any band comprised the wives of the men and possibly a few unmarried girls, close to puberty. These single women were each related to one or more of the men in the group; either their father or a brother was a member of the same local clan. The married women of this Boon wurrung foraging party probably came from one of the Watha wurrung clans, groups with whom the Boon wurrung were most closely aligned.

Although hunting was generally the prerogative of men, women could and did catch small animals whenever they happened upon them. Young children also soon learned to capture lizards, kangaroo rats, small mammals and grubs; these animals often made up part of the daily fare. During the day's collecting, the women and children might stop to cook some of their catch as a midday meal. The small mounds made by the discarded shells from shellfish form what are called middens, but these lunchtime piles were generally too small to survive for many years.

By early afternoon the women would have collected enough shellfish and vegetable foods to provide for most of the group. During the day the women might also have collected small empty shells washed onto beaches, for use in making necklaces. These shells are threaded onto twine in lengths up to three metres, which are worn wound around the neck. When the women

This composed picture of Port Phillip Koories from 1849 illustrates many of the major elements of Aboriginal personal equipment: possum skin cloaks, digging sticks, string bag, throwing stick and boomerang.

arrived back at the camp they first gathered wood to rekindle the fires. Water also needed to be brought from the freshwater stream; this was a job for the children who would use wooden bowls or buckets made from the gnarled section of a tree trunk to carry the water back to camp. These buckets were called tarnuks and there were several types, including one that had rope handles.

In all Koorie clans there were specific rules regarding the way in which particular animals were cooked and who received which portion when these animals were captured. These rules took into account aspects such as the species of animal to be distributed, who had made the kill, and which members of his family were present in camp. For example, if the man who made a kill was accompanied by another in the taking of a large animal such as kangaroo, emu and wallaby, the game was usually gutted and cooked at the scene. The meat was then divided between the two, with the hunter getting a forequarter, and a portion being reserved for his parents. The man's companion could take the other forequarter and the rest was divided among other members of the band. These rules apply particularly for the larger game. However, if a man or woman returned to camp with only enough for their immediate family, arrangements were made to ensure that others were also provided for—nobody went hungry in an Aboriginal camp. If there were dingoes in camp, they were fed the leftover bones.

Shellfish was cooked in the ashes of a well-tended fire but the cooking of a large animal such as a wallaby was rather more involved. A fire pit was dug and a number of stones put in the embers. When these were hot they were covered with green boughs and the carcass placed on top. This was then covered with a sheet of bark and loose earth was used to seal it up. In preparing the wallaby for the oven, the intestines, sinews and claws were removed and set aside (the skin was not removed unless it was needed for another purpose) to be used later.

After eating the fish, the shells of these mussels and scallop were discarded in a heap near the campsite. Bones from animals that had been cooked also ended up on this rubbish heap, which over a period of days or weeks led to a sizeable pile. In a campsite that was repeatedly and regularly used, these shell heaps or middens could grow to form a huge mound of about 40 cubic metres.

While the food was cooking the men set to fixing their kits of implements and hunting equipment. When a man's spear needed barbs replaced he makes them quickly from flakes struck from a core of stone material, using a hammer-stone. The process of flaking stone created a lot of small waste flakes on the ground that could puncture bare feet. For this reason there was often a designated 'workshop' area in the campsite, where this work was done. The men made these flaked tools on a daily basis and for an experienced knapper of stone, it took only a few minutes to make a new spear barb. Often, the finished object required a bit of further reshaping, and then it had to be fixed to the spear shaft with gum, and perhaps bound on with animal sinew. The right sort of gum was not widely available in Boon wurrung country and so a wad of the substance was often carried by the men for that purpose. Other domestic duties such as carving a wooden bowl, fire-sharpening a spear or repairing an animal hide were done at this time.

In the camp the children played: boys often practised their throwing skills in imitation of the men's hunting activities; girls played string games, and spent time with their mothers or aunts learning to construct baskets and bags.

When the sun dipped below the horizon, people turned in around fireplaces. At warmer times of the year, particularly if the nights were still, there was no need for huts or shelters and people lay protected by the natural depressions in the sand dunes.

## Shifting camp

After a few days of being at the same site the women might find that it is becoming harder to collect sufficient shellfish, or the men find that game was becoming harder to snare. To move to a new site, which might be as much as ten kilometres away, everyone had to gather together their portable belongings. The location of the new camp was always agreed upon beforehand, because the party would split up for the day's foraging on the way to the new site.

Aboriginal toolkits and most equipment were light and portable.

Women took their digging sticks, bowls, baskets and bags. Heavier objects such as wooden buckets, grinding stones and mortars and pestles, were generally not carried from site to site (unless the next camp was quite near) but stashed in a convenient hiding place, to be taken up again the next time the group returned to the site.

The men also travelled light, carrying only their hunting equipment and personal items like hammer-stones and hatchets. Small items were carried in a kangaroo-skin bag.

On striking camp, the men headed off into the bush on a roundabout course that would bring them to the new campsite in the middle of the afternoon. They might collect some stone for making tools from a small outcrop that they know in the vicinity and, of course, kept an eye out for animal tracks to assess how much game there was in the area.

The women moved more directly towards their new site, although they would collect plant foods and capture any small animals that crossed their path. Their route might have taken them along a well-worn track, made from repeated trips through the same piece of land.

This Boon wurrung band headed north into an area where there were few freshwater streams. By keeping to the track, the women would have passed a number of places where they could collect fresh water. There was a particular track that ran along the margin of the bay, close to the beach. In the Black Rock/Beaumaris area it passed a number of natural freshwater wells in the red sandstone. The wells provided access to the underground water table, but because they were covered by high tide twice daily they had to be cleaned out before use. In a short time, however, a good quantity of fresh water seeped into the hole from the water table. This natural feature still exists, close to the Beaumaris Yacht club. Water does not flow as easily into the well now because the water table has been lowered by overuse of water since white settlement.

Similar wells exist in a number of estates of Eastern Kulin clans, and also in Watha wurrung territory. Near the Werribee River, for example, there is a well, about a mile from its mouth that was also used by the first party of Europeans to explore the Port Phillip region in 1803. And in the You Yangs there is a natural depression on Big Rock, which collects water and which was used as a source by local people.

By the early afternoon the women would have arrived at the new site, and started setting up the campfires to cook the main meal of the day. The men would have arrived later with the results of their day's work.

If it looked like being a cold or wet night the men would have built simple lean-to shelters. Using stone hatchets, sheets of bark about two metres long were stripped from nearby trees and leaned on a framework of tree branches. Altogether, it took less than an hour to put up a 'village' of miams, each big enough to hold about five people. By overlapping the sheets of bark the shelter was made waterproof, but these structures were for temporary use only, during inclement weather.

CHAPTER FIVE

# A large camp at the Bolin Wetlands

Before the European invasion disrupted their way of life, Eastern Kulin clans moved freely around their estates on an annual cycle. Movement was a central aspect of Koorie life but it was far from aimless or random. People travelled to take advantage of available resources, fulfilling spiritual obligations, and engaging in ceremonial and ritual activity at significant sites. As the white settlers increasingly occupied the land along the Yarra, it became impossible for the Woi wurrung to continue to live as they had done for hundreds of generations. Within four years of John Batman's arrival there were European settlers all along the southern side of the Yarra, from the small township of Melbourne to Yering in the Yarra Valley. All across Eastern Kulin land, Koories were denied access to resources such as the plant food sources they had long relied on, as the new landowners objected to them moving through their pastures. At the same time, these food sources diminished, as the settlers' livestock destroyed much of the native vegetation.

Fishing at night involved using a lighted brand held near the water, to attract the fish, which are then more easily speared. This scene depicts a group at work on the Merri Creek, in the Plenty Ranges.

In pre-European times, the changing seasons were a major influence on how the people lived. The Woi wurrung lived in all parts of their territory

Rock wells such as this one at Ricketts Point on Port Phillip Bay are natural features that act as sources of fresh water. In some instances these rock formations have been modified to assist water to flow into the well. This well was supplied from the water table but needed to be cleared of sand before use.

from Mount William near Lancefield, across the tributaries of the Yarra to the Dandenong Ranges. In time-honoured fashion the foraging bands of Wurundjeri spent the warmer months on the banks of the lower Yarra and its tributaries. As the days became cooler, these groups moved up to higher land—into the Dandenong Ranges—where there would be more shelter and abundant firewood. On their way to the Ranges they would stop at significant places along the Yarra—one of these was a large wetland complex they called Bolin. The locals knew that at the time they were moving upstream towards more sheltered areas, mature eels were moving in the opposite direction, making their way downstream to breed in salt water.

The Koories had been keen observers of the natural world for thousands of years and were sensitive to subtle shifts in the landscape and climate that heralded seasonal change. The appearance of eels in the main waterways and billabongs was a signal to begin moving towards the higher land of their estates. The seasonal occurrence of an abundant food source such as the migration of eels was also an occasion for larger gatherings, mostly to do with maintaining the connections between related but often-distant clans. Every year, for hundreds of generations as many as 200 people spent up to four weeks at a time at this wetland and they continued to do this for some years after the arrival of Europeans in the Eastern Kulin estates.

It's no surprise then that these occasions often led to a series of camps being formed. It was common for members of different clans to camp together. After the sites were chosen and huts established, a series of ceremonies would take place in the surrounding area for a week or more. These ceremonies were to initiate those youths who had come of age, into the clan. This was a good time and place to have ceremonies of this kind because there was plenty of food. And there were other places in other tribal territories. The Watha wurrung clan that took in William Buckley, the escaped convict, lived for months at a time in one area near Lake Corangamite in the Western District. Just as at Bolin, when local bands gathered there, eels were a staple foodstuff; Buckley even described using a line with worms as bait to catch the eels.

Eels were caught in various ways at Bolin and in the many other swamps and lagoons around the land of the Eastern Kulin. Sometimes they were speared, using a wooden spear tipped with the peduncle or stalk of the grass tree. George Robinson wrote of hunters who held two spears in their hands while they sought out the eels with their feet. The eel was jabbed and removed from the water with one spear and then killed with the other. They also could simply be captured by hand. The best way to locate the eels in the wetland was to wade into the water, where they could be felt with the feet or seen. At this time of year eels were plentiful; two men could catch as much as twenty kilograms in a short time without having to go far.

The men who went fishing used a net made from the fibre of stringybark and spun into cords. This would have been stored in a hollow log from their previous visit. On arrival, the net would have been inspected and repaired, if needed, before the party set off.

Fish hooks were not commonly used in the Port Phillip area but there was more than one way to catch a fish. At a number of places around the region there were traps set in rivers and streams, at points where the flow of water was restricted. Funnel-shaped fishing pots take the fish as they swim with the stream. John Batman saw one of these on the Barwon in 1835 and another was seen in 1803 at what has become known as Solomon's Ford on the Maribyrnong River, near Avondale Heights.

At night, in bark canoes on the river the men held lighted brands near the water's surface. Freshwater fish such as Australian Grayling (*Prototroctes maraena*) and Tupong (*Pseudaphritis urvillii*) were attracted to the light and more easily speared. These spears were often tipped with a bone point. Sometimes the Boon wurrung caught fish in the bay, just offshore at night, in the same way.

The canoes used were simple craft, made from a single sheet of bark stripped from a tree, usually a River Red Gum, using a stone hatchet. The natural curve of the bark was accentuated by heating it over a fire so that the sheet turns up on both ends. The canoes were large enough to carry two or three men, and sufficiently stable to allow a man to stand up and spear fish. These canoes, however, were not often used on the more open waters of the bay.

As the days became longer and warmer, people moved back down the river valleys to camp again at the many wetlands, when the birdlife was

This scene of Koories bathing in the Yarra is more interesting for its composition than for what it can tell us about Eastern Kulin life. No doubt people bathed, swam and in hot weather cooled off in the many streams. And, as this scene implies, mothers watched over their children carefully as they played in the water.

particularly plentiful. At these times there was a good supply of birds' eggs and the birds themselves were also caught and eaten—a welcome change from eels—although more difficult to catch.

This time of year was also when the greatest number of perennials was available. Around the wetlands and marshes the young shoots and roots of bulrush (*Typha* sp.) were picked for eating, as were the tubers of Water Ribbons (*Triglochin procera*) and the roots of Common Reed (*Phragmites australis*). The women also collected rushes such as the Spiny-headed Mat-rush (*Lomandra longifolia*), which they take back to the camp and use to make baskets. Items of personal adornment such as necklaces were made from Common Reed.

During the day the women also gathered tubers from local plant species, such as stands of Sea Club-rush (*Bolboschoenus caldwellii*), which were roasted in an earth oven then pounded into thin cakes, before eating. The stone implements used for this process were too heavy to be carried from camp to camp and so were stored close by the Bolin wetlands. Utensils similar to these were used also for grinding the seeds of some plants and, prior to some ceremonies, for grinding ochre.

One of the more favoured plant foods was called Murnong (*Microseris lanceolata*); it grew most abundantly in spring and summer, especially on grassland plains, red gum woodlands and dry sclerophyll forests of Eastern Kulin territory. In the early days of settlement it was noted as being abundant along the banks of many streams, particularly the Moonee Ponds and Merri creeks. The tuberous perennial had yellow petals and looked something like a dandelion, which led to its European names, Yam daisy and Native Dandelion. It was an important food source because of its tuber and because it was readily available. The women dug up the plants and the tuber was roasted or eaten raw.

In some parts of Woi wurrung territory, particularly the Sunbury area, women were observed regularly turning over the mounds of soil in which Murnong grew. Actions of this kind can be seen as plant husbandry and are in keeping with a range of practices by Aborigines in other parts of Australia.

Across Victoria as a whole, there were almost 300 plants whose roots or tubers were eaten by Koories; among the more important, in addition to the Yam daisy, were many species of lilies and orchids. In grasslands and

Camouflage was the primary strategy used to approach game. Men hid behind specially made portable devices, hand-held foliage and more permanent hunting hides.

open woodlands, Koories managed and tended to these resources, principally through the use of fire. At regular intervals of three to five years, fire was applied to areas within their estate, as part of the practice of caring for their country. Soon after the burning, the women would go through the area, digging out the tubers from the burnt perennials. This digging had a number of outcomes: the removal of the underground parts of the plants served to aerate the soil, it mixed the ash into the humic layer, and it thinned out the surrounding vegetation. The net result of all this activity was that in the following year, when the foraging bands returned to the area they could expect an increased 'crop' of tubers, providing a ready source of foodstuffs. Over the following three to four years, however, the yield of tuberous species of orchids and lilies and other annuals would decline, until the process was repeated.

These practices, referred to by archaeologist Rhys Jones as 'fire-stick farming', had other impacts on the land of the Eastern Kulin. The vegetation cover in those areas where fire was regularly applied was maintained at a level of open woodlands and grasslands, regimes most useful to Koorie economic practices. The grasslands that stretched to the west and north away from the Maribyrnong River, and the open red gum woodlands across the north of the settlement were the result of these Koorie management strategies. In both instances the regular burning inhibited the spread of shrubs and trees. As well as allowing more sunlight to fall on the herbs and wildflowers growing at ground level, it made travel through these areas easier, and provided greater vision across the landscape. The firing promoted new growth of grasses, which in turn attracted game to the area, and helped the men hunt. Fire was occasionally used also as a way of driving game out of hiding in the grass and shrubs.

This drawing of the Yam Daisy or Murnong (*Microseris lanceolata*), shows the flowers that resemble dandelions, the leaf structure and the tuber, which was an important food source for Eastern Kulin clans. The herbaceous species was one of hundreds of plants used by Koories within Victoria.

## Back at the camp

By mid-afternoon everybody would have returned to the campsite with their respective hauls. Those who had gone in search of possums returned with a large number of Brush-tailed Possums (*Trichosurus vulpecular*). The men first set about taking off the pelts before the animals were cooked in the earth

oven. Most of the skins would later be used for making cloaks but the animals that were beginning to moult were consigned to the oven with the skin intact.

There were times when Boon wurrung groups preserved possum carcasses and dried them out over the fire. The entrails were first removed and the animal was slowly dried so that it would keep for longer and provide meat on some journey into territory that was poor in resources. In much the same way, Kangaroo Rats were also dried, and kept for leaner times.

Possums were relatively easy to catch. The trees in which they lived were identified by tell-tale scratch marks. In climbing the tree, toe-holds were cut into the trunk using a stone hatchet; this implement was kept handy because sometimes a hole had to be opened in order to get the possum out. If the possum was difficult to catch, a fire was lit at the bottom of the tree and smoke was used to drive them out.

After the skins were removed from the possums, the women began the first stage in the long process of making a possum skin cloak. It could take many days, depending on the number of skins available at the time. About eighteen skins were needed to make a decent-sized cloak. The skins were then cut into squares of about 25 to 30 cm and stretched out on sheets of bark using wooden pegs to hold them fast. The inner side of the pelt was cleaned using a mussel shell or stone scraped, and when the skins had dried out lines were incised with a stone blade, to make the skin more flexible. The inside surface was treated with a mixture of red ochre and charcoal mixed with fat to provide further insulation. The skins were eventually sewn together with sinew or muscle fibre, the holes being punched with the long tooth of a kangaroo or a bone sharpened to a point. Designs were at times cut into the surface of the finished cloak to make it distinct and mark it as having been made within a particular clan.

These cloaks were highly prized, because of the skill and workmanship involved in making them, and because of the warmth they provided. When the clan moved up into the sheltered areas of the higher country the newly-made cloaks were taken along; as the weather improved and the group moved back towards the low country, the cloaks were rolled up and stored in a safe place close to a winter camp.

This painting, published in a German history of mankind in the 1880s was meant to illustrate aspects of Australian Aboriginal life. Thus there is a range of activities taking place; the making of a possum skin cloak, and the skinning of an animal. In the eyes of the artist, the adult male has assumed the position of lord and master and is overseeing all.

Tommy McCrae was an Aboriginal artist from the Upper Murray District. His drawing of Kulin people welcoming the first ships, is possibly a comment about the way in which the Kulin initially struck a deal with the whites. This is implied too by the presence in the drawing of two figures that could be clan-heads, providing authority to the event.

Fragments of a possum skin cloak were recovered during investigation of a cave site in Springfield Gorge near Lancefield in 1980. Conditions for preservation at the site were excellent and as well as the fragments of possum skin there were bundles of emu feathers and some cord made from fibre which date back some 330 years.

The fur from possum skins was also used to make a length of yarn, which was then rolled up into a ball and used in a game regularly played by Koories. The game was called Marn grook and consisted of kicking the ball of possum fur into the air and then attempting to beat the other players to catch it. The player who marks the ball then kicks it into the air again and the game continued. It is possible that Tom Wills, one of the founders of Australian Rules football saw this game being played in the Western District in the 1860s, though if he did, it is unclear whether or not it influenced his thinking on football.

## Corroborees

As a gesture of welcome to the visitors from other groups who had come for the initiation ceremonies, a corroboree was performed one evening by the host clan. Corroborees were occasions when the dancers and singers could express their feelings about seeing their visitors, and perhaps tell a story which was part of their mythology—it was an occasion to demonstrate their imagination and inventiveness.

It was the men who performed the dance and in preparation, they would paint their bodies using white clay painting lines of large dots down the fronts of their legs, broad strokes on their torso and large open circles on their upper arms. The whiteness of the designs was highlighted by the campfires and gave a dramatic effect to the dance.

During the dances, the women chanted rhythmically, and produced a beat by drumming their hands on animal skins stretched tightly between their legs. Handclapping and the slapping together of sticks and boomerangs were also used.

There was nothing secret or sacred about these performances and they were held openly in many places around Eastern Kulin territory. In the estates of the Woi wurrung and Boon wurrung clans, corroborees were observed on Parliament Hill, Emerald Hill and the elevated area where Xavier College now stands in Barkers Road, Kew. These dance events were also witnessed close to the Merri Creek near Pentridge, in Collingwood near Victoria Park, and what is now Royal Park.

Two sites in Melbourne have been marked as reminders of these ceremonies. Next to an old River Red Gum in St Kilda Junction there is a plaque that notes that Koories corroboreed beneath and around the tree in the early days of the settlement. There is, however, no suggestion within records relating to corroborees of any importance attached to trees. A similar monument, without a plaque but fenced in, is in Richmond, close to Burnley Oval. This tree shows the marks of having had a sheet of bark removed at some time in the past.

## Private ceremonies

Unlike the public display of the corroboree, the details of ceremonies that took place for initiations or as part of totemic activity, were secret. The initiation of young men into full tribal status was performed in specific but secret places, away from the gaze of onlookers. These locations were not revealed to anyone who was not of the right clan or totem and entitled to witness the ceremony.

These activities often left no trace with which to later identify the site—the significance of a site for ceremonial purposes stems from its natural formation, not from what men have done to change it. There are some sites, however, that have been made ceremonial in nature by virtue of constructed rock arrangements. In the Sunbury area there is a group of sites—circular depressions with a central cairn of stones—that may have been used for ceremonial purposes. And there is a stone arrangement near Mount Rothwell to the west of Geelong that may also have been used for ceremonial purposes.

Because the disruption of the Eastern Kulin way of life was so rapid and dramatic we know very little about the spiritual aspects of that life, we can reasonably assume that it was complex and rich. Unfortunately, few Europeans made meaningful enquiries about how the Eastern Kulin ceremonies were held, who participated and what was being celebrated or mourned. Even within Kulin clans, it is likely that some ceremonies were known only to those people directly involved: initiation rites were the property of those who had been initiated and women conducted ceremonies known only to them. What *is* known is that the Kulin, like Aboriginal people all over Australia, believed that they were an integral part of the land. In the Koorie world, nature and culture had begun in the same acts of creation performed by ancestral beings. Everything that Aboriginal people did, including their hunting and gathering and the management of their country, was an expression of their spiritual life.

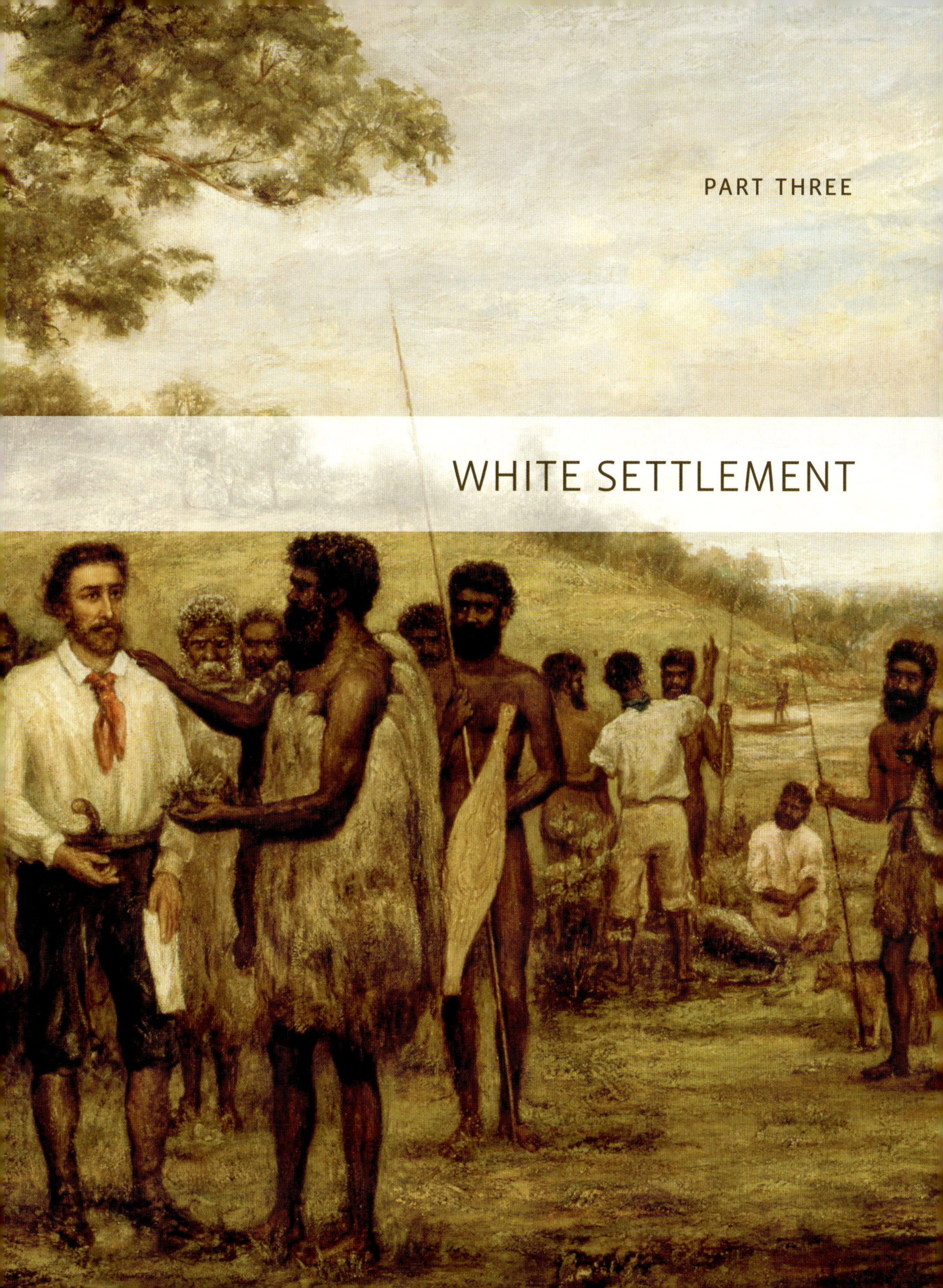

PART THREE

# WHITE SETTLEMENT

CHAPTER SIX

# The impact of White Settlement

From the mid–1830s onwards the clan estates of the Eastern Kulin were invaded in a wholesale way, from both the north and south. The Kulin called these strangers *Ngamajet*. The word also means the bright red colours at sunset; the place where the sun sets is *Ngamat* and the coloured sky is the place where departed spirits go. Because the strangers' skin was white, they were initially thought to be returned spirits.

Koories were aware of these strangers long before they began to appear in increasing numbers, because white people had trespassed on Eastern Kulin land many times from the beginning of the nineteenth century. Yet none of those sightings had led to a permanent presence by Europeans or gave any indication to the Kulin clans what was to follow.

From the end of the eighteenth century, small groups of sealers had operated around the southern coast of the continent, from bases on some of the Bass Strait islands. It is probable that from time to time these men also landed on the mainland, particularly in Gunai country to the east of Wilsons Promontory. Certainly, the coastal areas of Boon wurrung territory

**Previous & Left**
John Wesley Burtt titled this painting 'Batman's treaty with the aborigines at Merri Creek, 6th June 1835'. While the date is certain, the precise location of the event has been a matter of debate ever since. The painting itself owe more to convention than to historical accuracy.

were explored by Europeans in the earliest years of the nineteenth century. This began with the first voyage of the *Lady Nelson* under Lieutenant James Grant in March 1801, during which Westernport Bay was visited, followed by a second excursion under Acting Lieutenant John Murray, where the *Lady Nelson* became the first ship to enter Port Phillip Bay in February 1802. During a stay of about three weeks in the southern region of the bay, an altercation between members of the ship's crew and a group of Boon wurrung resulted in two Koories being killed.

Late in April 1802, about eight weeks after the *Lady Nelson* had departed, Matthew Flinders arrived in the *Investigator*, thinking he was the first European to do so. During his brief stay he explored the bay's northern margin, climbing the highest peak of the You Yangs, before departing on 3 May. In January and February of the following year a detailed survey of the perimeter of the bay was carried out by a party from the *Cumberland*. It was during this expedition, directed by Charles Grimes, Surveyor General of New South Wales, and aimed at assessing the prospects of the region as a site for future settlement, that the Yarra River was first navigated by Europeans. In almost two months, as they walked the entire margin of Port Phillip Bay, the Grimes party had only minimal contact with Koories.

In the opinion of James Flemming, gardener and expedition diarist, there was only one location that was eligible for settlement, which was on the 'Freshwater' river. At the same time two ships were about to leave England bound for Port Phillip, carrying a large party of convicts and free settlers. Following his receipt of the separate reports of Murray and Flinders, Governor King in Sydney had suggested establishing a British presence in the area, to forestall what he saw as French colonial interests. The two ships—HMS *Calcutta* and the *Ocean*—arrived in early October 1803 and the convicts, soldiers and settlers, under the direction of Lieutenant Colonel David Collins, set about creating a settlement at Sorrento.

In the earliest days of this incursion into Kulin territory, Lieutenant James Tuckey carried out a reconnaissance of the top of the Bay; unfortunately, he was unable to manoeuvre his boat into Hobson's Bay and so missed seeing the mouth of the Yarra River. While exploring the northern end of Corio Bay,

Tuckey's party encountered a group of about 200 Koories. Tuckey, feeling threatened, had his men fire on them, killing at least one man and injuring several more. Writing about the episode later, Tuckey commented that the Koories *'appeared to have a perfect knowledge of the use of fire-arms'*. If they didn't know about firearms before that encounter, they certainly did after it.

The site chosen by Collins for a settlement was not a suitable one, through a lack of fresh water and poor soils, and in December 1803 he received permission to relocate. Given a choice between Port Dalrymple (Launceston) or the Derwent, both in Van Diemen's Land, Collins decided to join Lieutenant John Bowen at the new settlement on the Derwent River. The last members of the Collins expedition were removed on 20 May 1804. Among the legacies this failed attempt at settlement left for the Kulin clans of the area was the enduring presence of William Buckley, one of a group of convicts that had escaped on Christmas Day, 1803. Buckley made his way to the other side of Port Phillip Bay and was taken up by a Watha wurrung clan, with which he lived until 1835.

Given the social and religious networks that existed across the world of the Eastern Kulin, there can be no doubt that Taung wurrung and Ngurai-illam wurrung clans living north of the Dividing Range were aware of what was happening around Port Phillip Bay and in 1824, a small group of Europeans passed through estates owned by Taung wurrung-speaking clans. The exploring party, consisting of Hamilton Hume and William Hovell and six convicts, entered Eastern Kulin country from the east, in their search for a route to Westernport Bay. Near present-day Seymour the party turned to the south and, crossing the Dividing Range, passed into Woi wurrung territory. Two months after leaving Hume's property near Lake George the party camped on the shore of Port Phillip Bay, near the site of Lara. They believed they had reached their destination, Westernport Bay.

Two years later, William Hovell actually did reach Westernport Bay—as a member of the expedition to establish a settlement in that area. This invasion of Boon wurrung country lasted longer than the Collins expedition more than 20 years earlier, and led to a wider exploration of the hinterland. As with the earlier attempt at creating a permanent settlement, however, the location was

Corroborees were usually held at major meeting of two different groups. The performance of song and dance was meant to convey a story and to impress the audience with its inventiveness. Corroborees were often held on successive nights in a spirit of competiveness, as each group would try to outperform the other.

not suitable—again because of poor soils and lack of fresh water. By early 1828 it had been decided, initially in Sydney and then in London, that the settlement party of twenty soldiers, twenty convicts and a few soldiers' wives should be withdrawn. They arrived back in Sydney in April 1828.

For the first three decades of the nineteenth century the country of the Eastern Kulin was trespassed repeatedly by Europeans, sometimes resulting in the death or wounding of Koories and it is also possible that local people felt the impact of Europeans long before their territory was physically invaded, through the spread of disease. The effects of diseases such as smallpox were felt in areas at some distance from the point of initial settlement, long before the Europeans appeared in those areas. In 1803, members of the first European exploratory party in Port Phillip noticed what looked like smallpox marks on the face of a Koorie they met on the Bellarine Peninsula. Admittedly, a single sighting is insufficient evidence of the disease having reached this area prior to a European presence—the pock marks may have been due to an infection called *impetigo contagiosa* (native pock)—however, there is some evidence that smallpox swept through south-east Australia in 1829–32, along major river systems, where the largest indigenous populations lived. Aborigines had no natural immunity to infections like smallpox, so the death rate in areas where epidemics occurred, such as along the Murray River valley, was unusually high. It is estimated smallpox had a fatality rate of 50 per cent of those infected. In the early 1840s Chief Protector G.A. Robinson, wrote of the total extinction of some groups in what is now the Western District. In May 1841 he wrote that Worrup.mo.un.deen, an old Ure Goondeet man whose territory was the site of Portland, was the last of his tribe. From the age structure of the groups that Robinson met in 1841, it is likely that the epidemic occurred in that area around 1830.

As the pastoralists grew in number and spread out with their sheep and cattle, more and more areas became closed to the Koorie owners. Day-to-day foraging and hunting activities were obstructed as settlers denied Koories the free use of their own land. Large herds of sheep browsed on the plains, eating out many of the plants that were habitual sources of food, at the same time disrupting the way of life of the native animals.

Worse was to come: the very siting of the township of Melbourne struck at the heart of the Eastern Kulin world. By an unhappy coincidence, the area in which the township was created had for many generations been a meeting ground for the member clans of the Kulin; it provided a series of locations at which business had been customarily enacted. But within a short time, the environs of the growing township became barred to Koorie access; moreover, many important Koorie sites became defiled through the presence of Europeans and their stock. Without access to time-honoured and important sites with a range of significance, ceremonies that were designed to ensure the continuance of the Kulin world could not be performed—young men could not be initiated with the seclusion required—and vital resources could not be gathered. The combined effect of these impediments to customary practice was that before long Kulin clans were largely unable to fulfil their spiritual obligations in the management of their country. This trend was exacerbated by the rapidly declining population; men and women of importance were dying before their time, and knowledge was dying with them.

From First Contact there were conflicts between Europeans and Koories, conflicts which (in the long term) Koories could not win. Although there was a sustained guerrilla campaign within Kulin territory on the part of small groups of armed Koories in the early 1840s, such efforts could not prevail. The number of European police or military units that could be mobilised as well as their superior weaponry meant that retribution was often swift and extreme. Further, settlers were quick to make retaliatory raids against any Koorie aggression, with no thought given to law or justice. When two white shepherds were killed by Koories near the Werribee River in July 1836, a band of seven heavily armed men went in search of the culprits, which resulted in the death of ten Koories. This incident was perhaps the earliest of its kind that occurred in Kulin country yet it was replicated time and time again in the following years. In April 1838 seven assigned convicts driving sheep for the Faithfull Brothers were killed by Koories on Broken River, near the site of present-day Benalla. Two months later, in a pitched battle, possibly with the same group of Koories, a group of European squatters and their servants killed seven or eight of the Koories. Indeed, the 'Faithfull massacre' prompted

Assistant Protector of Aborigines William Thomas as sketched by George H Haydon in 1842. Haydon was an artist and art teacher who also sketched a number of Koorie subjects around the Melbourne area.

WT— AP.
Haydon.
1841

local squatters to undertake a number of reprisal raids, which resulted in the deaths of dozens of Koories.

The Koorie population across the Port Phillip District as a whole declined rapidly in the years following the European invasion. It is uncertain how many Koories there were at the time of settlement but estimates are in the order of 15,000. By 1863 the number had plummeted to 1907 Koorie individuals and by 1877 it had been further reduced to 1067. By Federation, in 1900, there were only about 650 Aboriginal people in Victoria. There are no precise figures for the Eastern Kulin but we do know that in the twenty-seven years following the foundation of Melbourne the number of Woi wurrung and Boon wurrung was reduced to twenty-eight.

A number of factors contributed to this decline in population. European diseases, to which the Kulin had no immunity, played a large part and one which was rapid in effect. Indeed, deaths from disease have been estimated as accounting for at least 60 per cent of the Aboriginal population of Port Phillip. Smallpox has been mentioned already but other introduced infections include influenza, tuberculosis, venereal disease, and pneumonia. Dysentery was also a problem, which in May 1839 caused a number of deaths among Koories in the Melbourne camp. The most common venereal diseases were gonorrhoea and syphilis; although these were not in themselves fatal they did weaken the sufferer's system and render people infertile.

George Robinson reported many instances of Koories who appeared to be suffering from venereal disease. It is not certain that he was correct in his assessment, however, because there were other afflictions, such as yaws, which had similar symptoms and were endemic to indigenous Australian populations. The major killer, however, was influenza. There was a number of epidemics of this infection among Koorie populations and one that began in June 1847 lasted for more than twelve months and led to the deaths of many people among the Woi wurrung, Boon wurrung, and Taung wurrung clans.

Another reason for the decline in Kulin numbers was a sudden and drastic reduction in birth rate. In the ten-year period from 1838, only five births were recorded for the Yarra and Westernport clans, while in the same period there were fifty-two deaths. The Assistant Protector William Thomas suggested that infanticide was increasingly practised, as Koories came to feel that there was no point in having children when they had been deprived of their land.

Consider the fatalism expressed by Derrimut, an *Arweet* or clan-head of the Yulakit willam clan of Boon wurrung speakers:

> *You see... all this mine, all along here Derrimut's once; no matter now, me soon tumble down... Why me have lubra? Why me have piccaninny? You have all this place, no good have children, no good have lubra, me tumble down and die very soon now.*

On another occasion, Billibellary, a clan-head *Ngurungaeta* of the Wurundjeri-willam clan of Woi wurrung speakers, commented that:

> *The Black lubras say now no good children, Blackfellow say no country now for them, very good we kill and no more come up Pickaninny.*

In January 1845 William Thomas noted that the Woi wurrung and Boon wurrung had no children under the age of five. The feelings of hopelessness and uncertainty about the future, as expressed by these clan-heads, are likely to have been a contributing factor to the greatly reduced birth rate following European settlement.

This portrait of the Boon wurrung clan-head Derrimut (or Derah Mat as the artist Benjamin Duterrau has it) was painted during a visit to Hobart in August 1836. Derrimut was a sometime employee of John Pascoe Fawkner and is credited with saving the young settlement on the Yarra by his warning of an impending attack.

CHAPTER SEVEN

# The Port Phillip Aboriginal Protectorate

## White settlement

When Batman travelled on the western side of Port Phillip Bay in May and June 1835, he carried with him a contract to 'buy' nearly a quarter of a million hectares from the local Aboriginal clans. This document had been drawn up beforehand by Joseph Gellibrand, a lawyer with Batman's Port Phillip Association. In exchange for their land the Koories around Port Phillip were to get twenty pairs of blankets, one hundred knives, thirty tomahawks, 200 handkerchiefs, thirty mirrors, fifty scissors, 100 pounds of flour and six shirts. Batman also agreed to pay a yearly rent of 100 pairs of blankets, 100 knives, 100 tomahawks, twenty suits of clothing, sixty mirrors, fifty scissors and five tons of flour for this land. Separate amounts of the same commodities were supposed to be paid for a large tract of land in the vicinity of Geelong.

The primary purposes of this somewhat fraudulent contract were twofold. Firstly, it was intended to show that the Port Phillip Association had legally acquired the land. The so-called treaty was based on a feudal form of land transfer called enfeoffment in which the deal had to take place on the

Following the closure of the Port Phillip Protectorate in December 1849, G A Robinson retired to live in England. This portrait was painted in 1853 during his subsequent grand tour of European cities.

land in question. Secondly, the enacting of the treaty sought to persuade the government in Sydney that the Port Phillip Association had treated the local Koories fairly and would continue to do so, and thus should be allowed to take up the acquired land. Prior to this, the government had been opposed to settlement by independent landowners in areas where there was no official presence. The action of the Port Phillip Association and others such as John Pascoe Fawkner forced the hand of the British government. In April 1836, the new settlement on the Yarra River was officially sanctioned and in the following September William Lonsdale was appointed Police Magistrate, and directed to take charge of the Port Phillip District of New South Wales.

Before Lonsdale's arrival, and part of the reason for his appointment, there were conflicts between Europeans and Koories in the Port Phillip region. The first occurred at Westernport Bay in March 1836 when a party of men employed to collect wattle bark fired on a group of Koories, wounding six. One of the injured was a young girl who was shot through both legs. In a letter to John Montagu, Colonial Secretary of Van Diemen's Land, Port Phillip Association surveyor John Helder Wedge reported that a similar attack had occurred about eighteen months previously, and on that occasion four women were kidnapped by the bark strippers. George Stewart, a Police Magistrate at Campbellfield, near Sydney, was sent to investigate but found that the guilty party had long since left the area. The second incident, also recorded by Stewart, occurred near the settlement early in 1836 when a stockman tried to rape an Aboriginal woman. The man was sent back to Van Diemen's Land by Batman and John Wedge.

## The Mission Settlement at South Yarra

From the very beginning of white settlement at Port Phillip, it was the intention of the British government to 'civilise' the Koories in that region. This was going to be done by inducing them to live together on a mission where they would adopt the European way of life and also be protected from conflicts with the white settlers. In order to do this, in early 1837 a mission station was set up under the control of George Langhorne, an Anglican missionary from Sydney.

The station consisted of about 362 hectares on the southern side of the Yarra River. The area selected for the mission included part of what is now the Royal Botanic Gardens. This site was chosen because it took in a hilly area where corroborees were held as well as a large wetland, rich in plant foods and wildlife. In the first months of setting up the mission and attracting Koories, Langhorne had the assistance of William Buckley.

It was Langhorne's plan to have the adults labour for a few hours each day. In return they would receive a portion of flour, beef or pork, tea, salt, sugar and soap. In the first months, however, not many Koories could be persuaded to take part in the scheme. Another aspect of the plan was to keep the children on the station and provide school lessons for them. The children were induced to stay with the promise of three meals a day if they did not leave without permission. Langhorne was keen to provide the children with a European education, and extra staff were engaged to carry out this task.

Over the first eighteen months of operation, attendance at the station by Koories—both adults and children—was irregular. Although the Koories' traditional way of life was already severely disrupted and access to their former areas was difficult, they clung to their customary patterns of movement. When they were in Melbourne they often came into conflict with the white settlers. The less respectable residents would incite the Koories to fight each other and would ply them with alcohol for their own amusement.

Langhorne had other problems, particularly with a man called Christiaan De Villiers. In October 1837 Lonsdale engaged De Villiers to form a Native Police Corps, which was to consist of Aboriginal troopers who would be used as a police force in the new settlement. Ideally, all the troopers would be from the same clan in order to minimise in-fighting. Langhorne began to question De Villiers's character and his activities. He claimed De Villiers was trying to ruin the efforts of the mission by drawing the adult men away to the police camp he had established on Dandenong Creek at Narre Narre Warren.

As a result of Langhorne's complaints De Villiers resigned in January 1838. The Koorie members of the Corps refused to work under anybody except De Villiers, and although Langhorne installed a resident manager at the Narre Narre Warren site, the scheme lapsed. The need persisted, however, and

De Villiers was reappointed months later in May, only to resign a second time in February 1839. This attempt at forming a Native Police force was then abandoned.

In the previous June, Langhorne had suggested the mission station be moved away from Melbourne, perhaps near Arthurs Seat on the Mornington Peninsula. This was not done, however, and by the end of 1838 all of his staff had resigned and Langhorne was left to work alone. As part of an economy campaign under New South Wales Governor Sir George Gipps, the positions at Langhorne's mission were not refilled. Indeed, very little money was made available for the mission's operations. The primary reason behind this was that the government had decided to scrap the Church of England mission and start a much larger and more ambitious scheme called the Aboriginal Protectorate. George Langhorne resigned in March 1839 and his mission in South Yarra was taken over in the same month by the new department.

## The Aboriginal Protectorate

The push for an official department such as the Aboriginal Protectorate grew out of pressure exerted by a reform movement based in London. The Anti-Slavery Society, having achieved their aim in 1833, and other reform groups turned their attention to 'civilising' the Indigenous peoples of British colonies, with the central tenet that conversion to Christianity was the natural means of achieving this goal.

In part the impetus for a Protectorate system was fuelled by an alarming increase in conflicts between Europeans and Koories in the Western District and closer to Melbourne. In May and June of 1838 there were conflicts between Koories and squatters in the area of Mount Macedon. A hut of one of the squatters was pillaged, a number of sheep stolen, and one of the shepherds killed. In a subsequent battle lasting about forty-five minutes, an unknown number of Koories, later estimated at seven or eight, were shot dead. The Native Police under De Villiers investigated the incident but did not find the Koories responsible for the murder of the shepherd; no attempt was made to prosecute the Europeans for their response to Koorie aggression.

There was a need for conciliation between Europeans and Koories, and a British House of Commons committee decided that an Aboriginal Protectorate was the answer. After much letter writing and consideration by politicians, the Protectorate was established with an initial staff of five men—a Chief Protector and four Assistants. The Chief Protector was to be based in Melbourne and assume responsibility for the administration of the department. Each of the Assistants was to settle in a specific part of the District with the intention of attracting local Koories to settle on his station. In practice some of the Assistant Protectors instead took to travelling with the Koories in that area in the hope of winning their confidence.

The Chief Protector was George Augustus Robinson, a fifty-one-year-old man who, between 1829 and 1835, had been instrumental in having the Tasmanian Aborigines removed from their land to Flinders Island in Bass Strait. While presiding over their rapid decline, as Commandant of the island mission, he refused an invitation to head a similar department in the recently founded settlement of Adelaide, apparently because he felt the salary of £250 per annum was too low. He was offered £500 per year to take up the position at Port Phillip.

Robinson's experience with Aborigines in Van Diemen's Land had made him the obvious choice to head the new department. His method of conciliating with the Indigenous people in that colony had been to travel into the territory of the Aborigines with Aboriginal companions who were prepared to act as go-betweens. In this way he had been able to persuade almost all the surviving groups of Tasmanian Aborigines to leave their land and be sent to Flinders Island. Robinson's actions in the District suggest that he believed the same method could be made to work in the Port Phillip settlement.

The four Assistant Protectors arrived by ship from England via Sydney in January 1839. With them came their wives and a total of twenty-two children. None of the Assistant Protectors had had any experience with Australian Aborigines. Three of the men were Wesleyan schoolmasters William Thomas, aged forty-three; James Dredge, forty-one; and Edward Parker, thirty-six and the fourth, an army officer of 'ungentlemanly reputation' was Charles Sievwright, thirty-six.

The Protectorate began its operations very slowly. In the early months of 1839 a great deal of time was spent arguing about the duties and rights of their respective positions; indeed, some of the Assistants seemed reluctant to depart from Melbourne at all. Sievwright was assigned the Portland Bay district but it took him two years to move past Geelong. Parker moved north-west towards the Loddon River but set up initially on Jacksons Creek, near present-day Sunbury. Dredge was given the Goulburn River district and Thomas was to look after the Koories of the Melbourne, Westernport and Gippsland areas.

George Robinson was a difficult man to please. Although he was essentially Melbourne-based, his lack of faith in the Assistant Protectors' abilities, together with an exaggerated opinion of his own, led him to make a number of journeys into the bush over the next ten years.

On a number of occasions Robinson was called upon to investigate reports of violent clashes between Koories and whites and took to the field to do his Assistants' work. Robinson's diary records cases where whites clearly killed blacks, with no charges laid. He complained of the inadmissibility of evidence by Koories in the courts. In the early months of 1840 Robinson travelled with Assistant Protector Parker in a reconnaissance of central Victoria to decide on a suitable location for Parker's Protectorate station. In the following year, from March to August he travelled through the Western District, from Melbourne to Portland Bay and back. During this trip he made contact with many Koorie groups and attempted to persuade them to settle on the Mount Rouse Station established by Sievwright.

The most valuable result of Robinson's travels for us today is his journal. Written during his various treks through the countryside, this has been an unparalleled source of information about a Koorie lifestyle barely touched by European settlement but which, within a few years was almost totally altered and destroyed.

Most of the information we have on the Boon wurrung and much on the Woi wurrung and Taung wurrung comes from Robinson's journal as well as the journals and papers of William Thomas, the Assistant Protector for the Westernport and Gippsland areas. The official records compiled during the Protectorate period also have been of great use in Koorie studies.

By the late 1830s, and increasingly in the following decades, Koories were seen by the authorities as a nuisance and a disturbing influence on the streets of Melbourne. Thomas spent a great deal of his time attempting to draw the Woi wurrung and Boon wurrung away from the settlement—to little effect. With the rapid influx of Europeans to the area, Koories found it increasingly difficult to maintain their customary practices, and to find food. In the face of these massive disruptions, most Koories tried to do everything they could to maintain their customary way of life; this often meant moving further and further away from the township of Melbourne. In some cases, their lives bereft of meaning, Koories became addicted to alcohol and, and in the absence of traditional food sources they resorted to begging. The European perception of a degenerate race was quick to develop, fanned by anti-Koorie elements in the local press. By the 1880s the city's remaining Koories were mostly seen as objects of ridicule or curiosity, to be displayed, for instance, at the Great Exhibition held in Melbourne in 1880–81.

Ultimately, the Port Phillip Aboriginal Protectorate was a failure and was closed down after ten years, on 31 December 1849. Part of the reason behind this failure must lie with the Assistant Protectors, who were unable to achieve the first aim of the scheme, which was to attract the Koories to their stations on a permanent basis.

The Koories in the area of Sievwright's Mount Rouse station disliked and avoided the Protector. He failed to gain the cooperation of local squatters, whom he reportedly treated in a high-handed manner. He was the subject of rumours of sexual impropriety, involving his teenage daughter Frances, and was also accused by his fellow Protector Edward Parker of making improper advances to Parker's wife. Sievwright was suspended by Governor Gipps on 3 June 1842, notionally on the grounds of misappropriating government stores, although his moral character must have weighed heavily on the governor's mind. The position of Assistant Protector for the Western District was then filled by Dr John Watton.

James Dredge resigned his post in June 1840, clearly aggrieved that he had been misled in London about the nature of his task. His replacement as Assistant Protector for the Goulburn River station was William Le Soeuf, who never managed a happy relationship with those Koories in his charge. Yet despite the widespread perception that he was afraid of the Koories, in the first eighteen months of his appointment he oversaw the development of agriculture on the station and managed to keep many local Koories occupied. Financial cutbacks during the depression of 1842–43 led to a reduction in station staff; though Le Soeuf was forced to resign in the latter part of 1843 when a range of irregularities in his management of government stores came to light. The position was not filled after Le Soeuf's resignation.

Edward Parker achieved a measure of success at his station near Mount Franklin and for a time had Koories regularly living there, where they tended crops and attended classes. The success was short-lived, however, although Parker stayed on as schoolmaster at the station when the Protectorate was dissolved. And Koories also remained on the station after December 1849, working it under the private direction of Parker. The station was finally closed in 1864 and the remaining residents transferred to Coranderrk, near Healesville.

William Thomas was perhaps the most successful of the Assistant Protectors, although he too had problems. The Boon wurrung were reluctant to settle at his station in Narre Narre Warren, which was the same site that De Villiers had chosen for the first Native Police Corps, in 1837, but the interesting thing is that it was within Woi wurrung territory. The Koories of Thomas's district were perhaps those most affected by the European invasion and they had the least chance of continuing their tradtional way of life. Thomas spent more time in travelling with the Koories of his district than his fellow Protectors, but he also spent a lot of time trying to stop them entering Melbourne. He also operated a school for Koorie children at the junction of the Merri Creek and Yarra River, from 1841 to 1851. (This site was also used as a second Protectorate station, during the decade of the Protectorate's operation.) When the Protectorate was wound up, Thomas was appointed Guardian of the Aborigines and continued to do his best for local Koories for many years.

Windberry, an important man in the Eastern Kulin, was the spokesman for Bebejan, clan-head of a Wurundjeri-willam patriline. He was killed while resisting a raid by military police on the Aboriginal camp in October 1840.

At first the Assistant Protectors were largely incapable of preventing clashes between Koories and settlers. In some cases they were even unable to prevent hostile action against Koories by other government officers.

No 1

In October 1840 a group of about three hundred Koories were surrounded in their camp on the south side of the Yarra, by a party of soldiers and mounted police led by Major Samuel Lettsom of the 80th Regiment. He was after a group of Goulburn Koories who were thought to be in the camp. The Koories were carrying rifles and were accused of a series of robberies in the northern district. A Woi wurrung clan-head, Windberry, was shot dead as he was about to defend himself. About 300 Koories were herded through the main street at gunpoint, prodded along by the bayonets and musket butts carried by the fifty-eight soldiers and police; another man was shot that night while allegedly trying to escape from the lockup. All but thirty were released on the same day, but the remaining prisoners were detained for a full month before ten of them were found guilty. One of the convicted men died in the prison and subsequently all but one escaped while being ferried down the Yarra, on their way to a ship bound for Sydney.

The reasons the Protectorate failed are manifold and include the people who had devised the scheme in London. With no direct experience of either Aboriginal culture or Australian conditions, they placed enormous expectations on the Protectors in the field. Other reasons for the failure of the Protectorate can be found in the government's lack of interest in the scheme once it was apparent that the 'Aboriginal problem' would not be easily solved and financial support was reduced. The Chief Protector and his Assistants were given no encouragement by squatters and even the press, with the exception of Fawkner's *Patriot*, was generally opposed to the scheme, and criticised every aspect of it. In an editorial on 3 July 1839 the *Port Phillip Gazette* claimed that the Protectors were unsuited to the tasks required, that the scheme was a waste of government money for no good purpose. The public was opposed to the principle of 'wasting a large portion of their emigration fund in a manner which the Colonial experience would have stamped as an act of reckless folly'.

Although the Koories were said to be equal before the law, clearly this was not the case. While the Europeans made sport of shooting native animals and their sheep ravaged the plant resources, thus destroying the basis of Koorie livelihood, the Koories themselves were shot or imprisoned for killing a sheep for something to eat.

In some respects, the Protectorate exacerbated the breakdown of traditional Kulin life: in dividing the Port Phillip District into four Protectorate areas, language groups were split between Protectors' districts. The Woi wurrung clans of the western side of Melbourne, Marin-bulluc, Kurung-jang-bulluc and Gung-willam-bulluc, for example, were grouped with Dja Dja wurrung clans from the area of the Loddon and Avoca rivers. They were thus administered separately from the other members of their language group, by a different Protector.

CHAPTER EIGHT

# Missions and Reserves

## Buntingdale Mission

For most of the time in which the Protectorate operated, from January 1839 to December 1849, there was also a mission to the Aborigines within the territory of the Eastern Kulin, funded and administered by a religious group. Established in June 1838, the Buntingdale Mission Station was situated on the Barwon River, near the present-day town of Birregurra, within Watha wurrung territory. It was operated by the Wesleyan Missionary under the direction of the Reverend Francis Tuckfield, who had selected the site. He was assisted in his ministry to the Koories by his wife Sarah.

The leader of the Wesleyan missionaries in Australia, Joseph Orton, had applied in May 1838 to the New South Wales government for a grant of 16 square miles (41.4 km$^2$) of land and funds to set up the station. Governor Gipps agreed to finance the venture but restricted the grant to one square mile.

The primary intent of the Mission was to convert local Koories to Christianity. Despite the best efforts of Tuckfield, who was at pains to learn the local language, the missionaries achieved little success, though perhaps it

Simon Wonga, pictured at the age of 37, was the son of Billibellary and—with his cousin, William Barak—one of the last Woi wurrung clan-heads.

As well as taking on the way of life of the whites Aborigines also took up their sports, including cricket. At about the time that Coranderrk was selected by the Eastern Kulin, an Aboriginal cricket team was formed in the Western District. This team toured England with some success in 1867–68.

is not surprising given his lack of understanding of his charges. In a letter to the Wesleyan Missionary Society in London in February 1839, he wrote of the Koories, 'their mind as it regards religion seems to be a rude chaos presenting an awfully distressing vacancy of thought'.

At the beginning at least Tuckfield and his assistant Reverend Benjamin Hurst were able to attract local people to stay on the station for protracted periods, but it was located close to a number of language groups, which led to conflicts; the resident groups expected the missionaries to take their side, which ran counter to the best interests of the Europeans. Hurst reported to Superintendent Charles La Trobe in May 1840 that—even in the first year of operation—a couple of serious conflicts occasioning bloodshed had occurred at the mission station. After an attack by about 200 Koories seeking revenge for a death which occurred in July 1841, local Koories largely deserted the station and the government withdrew its support after a few years. It was only by holding the station as a grazing licence that Tuckfield continued, but eventually even this licence was withdrawn and the station closed in 1851.

After the dissolution of the Protectorate, the government grouped all Koories together on mission stations and reserves. The Central Board for Aborigines was created in June 1860 and one of its earliest decisions was to settle Koories on supervised missions and government stations, where they could learn to farm and support themselves. A small number of stations already existed, including the former Protectorate station near Mount Franklin, where some Dja Dja wurrung Koories had become successful farmers.

Between 1858 and 1869 six new stations were set up across Victoria and a system of local Guardians instituted to oversee operations at each. Coranderrk, near Healesville, was established in 1863 and was where the Eastern Kulin clans gathered. Other stations included Framlingham (1866) and Lake Condah (1869) in the Western District; Ebenezer (1859) in the Wimmera; and Lake Tyers (1861) and Ramahyuck (1862) in Gippsland.

Through the 1860s and succeeding decades, Aboriginal people in Victoria were significantly better off than their contemporaries in other colonies. Not only did Victoria have a smaller Aboriginal population than most other colonies but because it was more closely settled, the 'frontier' phase had passed and Koories were regarded with more benevolence than in other colonies where violent conflict still occurred. Moreover, because of gold discoveries Victoria was a wealthy place that could afford to provide services to its indigenous people. Koories were clearly within the ambit of the legal and political system in Victoria, in a way that Aborigines in other colonies were not.

The creation of the Coranderrk station provides a rare example of Koories taking the lead in determining their own future but the process was a difficult one and took some years. In February 1859 seven Eastern Kulin men—two sons of the late Billibellary, a Woi wurrung clan-head, and five Taung wurrung men—asked William Thomas to appeal to the Victorian government on their behalf. They wanted a reserve of land within their country where they could live out their lives in freedom from European harassment. After a further deputation, this time to government ministers, in March it was agreed that an area of 4500 acres (1821 ha) could be chosen, just below the junction of the Little and Acheron rivers. A white overseer was appointed and four trustees nominated by Thomas. At first the scheme went well: eighty Kulin had settled on the Acheron station by December and crops were being planted, but thirteen months later all was lost to the Kulin.

Unfortunately, the four trustees Thomas had chosen were local squatters whose own interests were not served by the presence of an Aboriginal reserve. In September 1860 Peter Snodgrass, an influential squatter and one of the trustees ordered that the station be moved four miles upstream, to land of such poor quality that Europeans could not use it. For some time Taung wurrung people refused to move to this new site at Mohican, claiming the location was too cold. Although the station struggled on for another couple of years the Kulin were never happy there.

One of the Woi wurrung men living on the Mohican station was William Barak. He was born the son of Bebejan, a Woi wurrung clan-head, and was present at the meeting of Kulin men with John Batman in June 1835. Barak had been a member of the Native Police Corps under Captain Henry Dana in the 1840s, and became a leader of the Woi wurrung. Early in 1863, led by Barak and his cousin Simon Wonga, who had taken over from his father Billibellary as

A general view of the Aboriginal Mission Station at Coranderrk, photographed by Fred Kruger in 1880, about fifteen years after Kulin clans had settled on the site.

Woi wurrung clan-head, the Kulin walked off the station. The group of about forty Woi wurrung and Taung wurrung travelled through the Black Spur and in March 1863 reached a former camping place on Badgers Creek, within Woi wurrung territory. This site, named Coranderrk after a local plant that flowered around Christmas, was acceptable to the Kulin and in the following months set about establishing a farm on the 2450 acre (992 ha) reserve.

The manager of the station, John Green, who had travelled with the Kulin from the Acheron area to Coranderrk, recognised that the Koories were determined to transform their lives and allowed them an unusual amount of freedom to manage their own affairs. Under Green's direction and with the assistance of William Barak and Simon Wonga, the station prospered; the residents presented a model for future Koorie stations. By 1871 there were 140 acres (56.7 ha) under cultivation, in gardens and growing grain and hops. In the same year the station ran 400 head of stock (cattle and horses), which meant a further 2400 acres (971 ha) was added to the reserve in July 1866; and by 1875 there was six brick buildings and forty cottages. The produce from this farm won first prize at the Melbourne International Exhibition in 1872.

Up to 1872 the Board was supportive of Green and the Kulin residents of Coranderrk. But selectors moved into the area, anxious to acquire more land for farming; the Board came under pressure from politicians and various individuals to close the station. The Koories fought long and hard, however, to retain control of their land. After the death of Simon Wonga in 1874, his cousin William Barak had assumed the position of clan-head, *Ngurungaeta*. He actively opposed proposals to reduce the size of Coranderrk, as well as proposals to remove the residents to the Murray River. In 1874 Barak led a protest march on Parliament House; and in 1881 another march took place, covering the 60 km from Coranderrk to Parliament, because rumours had reached the Koorie residents that the station was to be dismantled. In both cases the political actions of the Kulin managed to save the Coranderrk reserve.

The struggle went on, however, and in 1893 half the area of the station was sold to outside interests. By 1924, when Coranderrk ceased to be a station staffed by the Board, most of the residents had been transferred to the Lake Tyers station in Gippsland and only nine elderly Koories remained behind.

The 1869 *Aborigines Act* originally was intended to protect Koories from mistreatment and exploitation by Europeans although it prescribed where Koories could live, restricted their movements, controlled how much they could earn and determined how the money allocated to Aboriginal services could be spent. While such measures were seen to be necessary in the 1860s, the legislation outlived the usefulness of these restrictions, and became a means whereby some members of the newly-reconstituted Board for the Protection of Aborigines (BPA) could exercise control over Koories.

The greatest threat to the successful operation of stations such as Coranderrk and Ramahyuck, however, came with the passing of the 1886 *Aborigines Act*, which became known as the 'half caste Act'. By the 1880s, with the Koorie population continuing to decline, the BPA changed its policy from one of maintaining the Koorie population in separate reserves to one of absorbing Koories into the general population.

The thrust of the 1886 Act was to remove all so-called 'half castes' from Board stations. Under this Act all Koories less than thirty-five years of age who were of mixed race were 'legally white' and could not continue to reside on Aboriginal stations. Across Victoria this amounted to half the estimated Koorie population of 844. As a result, the size of communities was halved by the removal and forced exile of the younger members. Farming became difficult if not impossible because not only was the labour force greatly reduced, but the majority of men left on the stations were too old for physical work.

The Act was particularly telling in its effect at Coranderrk, which had become a haven for many orphans of mixed parentage. Their removal from the station meant that those least able to support themselves were thrown into a white society on the brink of the economic depressions of the 1890s.

One impact of this legislation was the movement of people from Coranderrk to the Aboriginal station run by Daniel Mathews at Maloga, on the Murray River in New South Wales. Denied access to stations in Victoria, a number of Koories moved to live in the neighbouring colony. A connection with Maloga had existed for some time, since people from Coranderrk had visited that station in the 1870s. While there, they talked about what they had achieved in Victoria by direct action. A decade later, some of the Maloga residents were tired of Mathews' manner so, following the example set by the Coranderrk people, they petitioned the New South Wales government in 1881 for land of their own. This movement led in 1883 to the establishment of a reserve at Cumeroogunga, on the New South Wales side of the Murray, opposite Barmah. This station later became an important location for Victorian Koories.

In the 1930s a number of Koories from Cumeroogunga, some of whom had family connections to Victoria, became involved in political movements. William Cooper had grown up on Maloga; in 1933 he moved to Melbourne and subsequently helped found the Australian Aborigines' League (AAL). His first effort was to organise a petition to King George V, seeking intervention to prevent the extinction of Aboriginal people. In 1939 Cooper was the honorary secretary of the AAL; the treasurer was Douglas Nicholls. Nicholls was also a vice-president, along with Margaret Tucker, both of whom had come from Cumeroogunga. Bill Onus, another former resident of Cumeroogunga, was closely involved with the AAL in the 1940s. These people and many others laid the foundation for successful campaigns revolving around Aboriginal rights.

This photographic study by Fred Kruger of two Koorie men in a bark canoe is a picture of tranquility. The men are posed in the craft on the still waters of, probably, Badgers Creek, near Coranderrk.

PART FOUR

# HISTORY AND ARCHAEOLOGY

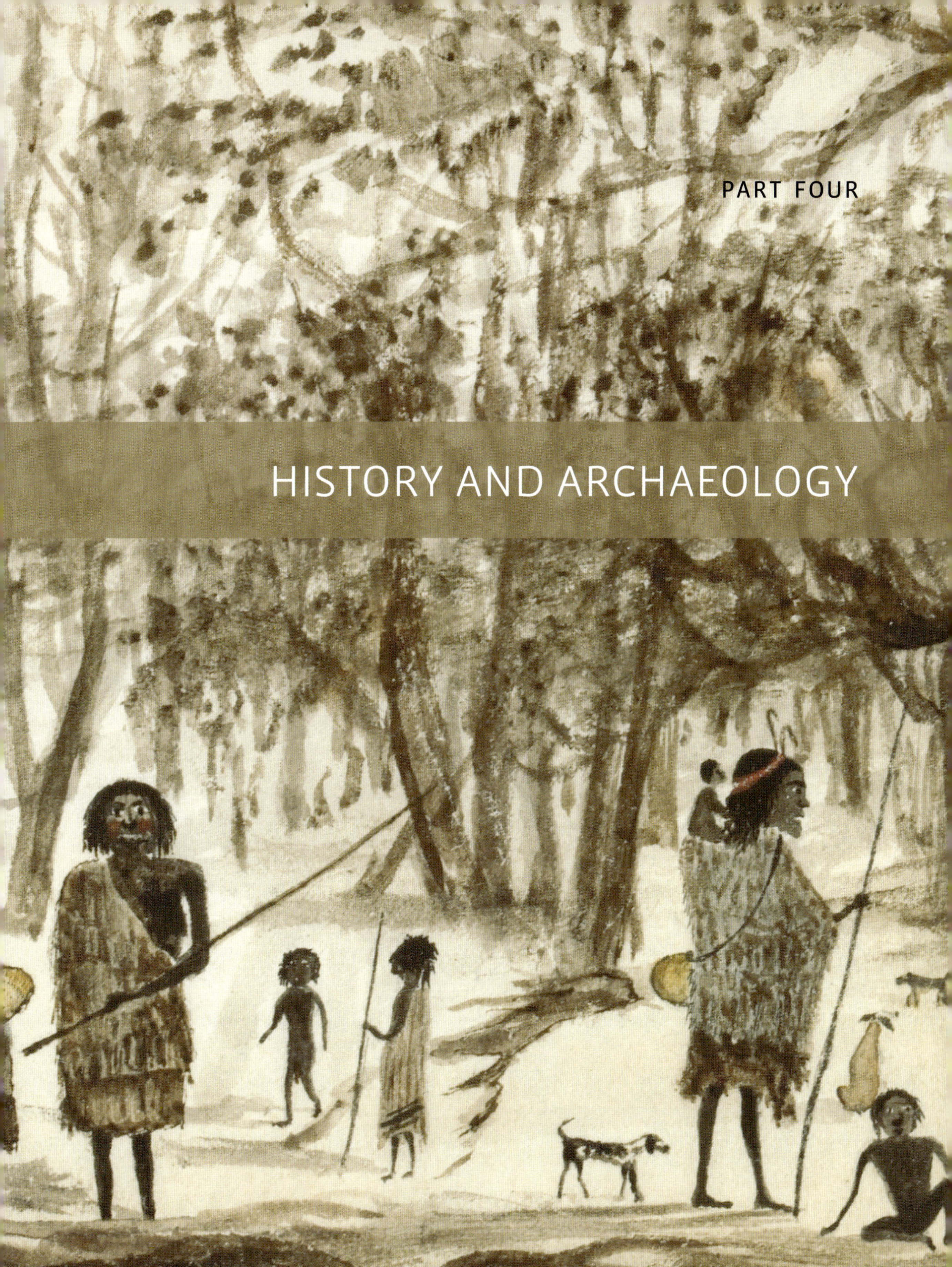

CHAPTER NINE

# Investigating the Past

The attempts to recreate the lifestyle and culture of the Eastern Kulin in this book have been drawn from information derived from geology, geography, botany, zoology, ethnography, history and archaeology. With regard to reconstructing aspects of the Eastern Kulin lifestyle and culture, it is perhaps with the last two—history and archaeology—that the weight of evidence lies.

Archaeology is a comparatively young profession in Australia but one that often captures the public imagination. It may be useful, then, to provide some detail about how archaeological studies have developed in the territory of the Eastern Kulin. The nature and intent of both archaeological and historical studies that are carried out at any given time, rest very firmly on the history of the discipline involved. Although they may not be the same, the ways in which archaeological sites, for example, are managed today has a relationship with how it was done in the past. Knowing how they differ reveals something about how far we have come in the development of understanding the past.

**Previous & Left**
This drawing of a group of women engaging in their customary collecting of foodstuffs provides some evidence of such activity. Note the presence of both young children and dogs. The former were being instructed; the latter would have been useful for chasing small animals such as antechinus and bandicoots.

## Archaeological beginnings

It was not until the mid 1960s that it was conclusively shown (through the use of radiocarbon dating) that people had been in Australia for a very long time. In 1962 the first radiocarbon date of more than 10,000 years before present was obtained—from a Queensland site called Kenniff Cave. This showed that the Aborigines had arrived in Australia before the end of the Ice Age. Prior to this find it was generally thought that the indigenous people of Australia had only a short and uneventful history in this country. By the end of the decade, however, there were sites dated in the range of 20,000 to 30,000 years ago, and now there are sites dated to more than 40,000 years ago.

From the 1930s onwards a few individuals, such as Norman Tindale at the South Australian Museum and Fred McCarthy at the Australian Museum in Sydney, had developed an interest in the Aboriginal history of Australia. Working from their bases in museums, these men and others carried out important studies of key elements of traditional Aboriginal culture, sometimes involving excavations. Detailed studies such as the 1929 excavations by Hale and Tindale at Devon Downs in South Australia, and McCarthy's 1936 excavation of Lapstone Creek formed the basis for the later, more systematic studies by trained archaeologists.

In Victoria, too, there were many individuals with interests in Aboriginal material culture, who researched and also collected artefacts. Through the 1920s and 30s Alfred Kenyon was a keen collector of stone artefacts, a passion he could indulge widely, as his duties as an engineering draftsman took him to many country localities. Kenyon was one of the first to suggest that Aboriginal sites should be protected by law. Stan Mitchell also collected a great deal of information over many years regarding evidence of the Aboriginal past in Victoria. He published *Stone Age Craftsmen* in 1949, which is now a classic of its kind. These men and their contemporaries formed what Tom Griffiths has characterised as a 'stone circle'. They were a close group of amateur ethnologists who were greatly influenced by the director of the National Museum of Victoria, Walter Baldwin Spencer, particularly by his views on stone tool classification.

Although professional archaeology was still more than three decades away, some archaeological excavation did take place in Victoria as early as the 1930s. Dermot Casey, a brother of Richard (later Lord) Casey and a highly experienced archaeologist, carried out a couple of digs on Aboriginal mound sites, including one in the Sunbury area. Casey worked with Edmund Gill, Deputy Director of the National Museum of Victoria (NMV) in digging a number of archaeological sites. Gill and other museum staff members, particularly from the anthropology department, were involved over many years with investigating and documenting past and present Aboriginal culture. Aldo Massola, Curator of Anthropology, wrote a number of books on the subject and contributed many articles to specialist journals. This work was continued by his successor at the museum, Alan West.

The chance discovery of a human cranium in a sand pit at Keilor in 1940 focused attention on the antiquity of humans in Australia, and the archaeological potential of the Keilor area. The age of the cranium (about 14,500 years) was not determined until the mid-1960s, by which time a complete human burial had been discovered at nearby Green Gully. This find drew interstate archaeologists to the area and one of these experts was John Mulvaney, who had recently taken up a post in the newly created archaeological department at the Australian National University in Canberra. Prior to that he had taught at The University of Melbourne for more than ten years and led a new front in archaeology in Victoria. Trained in archaeology at Cambridge University, John Mulvaney was the first university-trained pre-historian to make Australia his subject. During his period at Melbourne, although he wasn't teaching Australian archaeology or pre-contact history, he excavated a number of Aboriginal sites in Victoria and South Australia.

The area of Keilor subsequently became associated with the Archaeological Society of Victoria (ASV). The society was formed in 1965, following a series of lectures on Middle Eastern archaeology given by William Culican. Beginning in 1966 and continuing until March 1974, members of the ASV scratched away at sites along Dry Creek, near its junction with the Maribyrnong River, under the direction of Dr Alexander Gallus, a Hungarian-trained archaeologist.

## Protection of archaeological sites in Victoria

Interest in archaeology within Australia quickened during the 1970s and in Victoria there were two major developments. Firstly, in 1972 state legislation was enacted that gave protection to Aboriginal artefacts and sites. Secondly, the archaeology department at La Trobe University had its beginnings with the appointment in 1976 of two staff members.

The first Act of parliament specifically passed to protect Aboriginal sites and artefacts in Victoria was the *Archaeological and Aboriginal Relics Preservation Act* 1972. Under this legislation it was an offence to damage, deface or sell an Aboriginal relic. This applied in Victoria regardless of the point of origin of the artefact or relic. It was also illegal to disturb or excavate any land in Victoria for the purpose of uncovering or discovering a relic without a permit. The Act was amended in 1980 and 1984, in each case to provide wider and more stringent protection for relics of the Koorie past. The latter amendments made it an offence to possess any Aboriginal skeletal material and to collect or pick up any portable relic without permission.

Since the framing of the first legislation to protect Koorie sites and objects, there have been many changes in the field of Australian archaeology. The most interesting shift has been an upsurge of interest on the part of Koories in their own history and culture. There are now many individuals and communities playing an active part in developing this awareness of traditional ways through various activities such as taking part in field archaeology, writing their life stories and teaching their youth traditional skills. Most importantly, Koorie history is no longer the sole province of white historians; Koories are writing their history and compiling their own records of their past.

Professor Tim Murray, of La Trobe University Archaeology Department, writing about the development of Aboriginal archaeology in Australia, pointed out that:

> *The first generation of heritage preservation legislation . . . can now be seen to have mostly reflected the needs and interests of professional archaeologists and to have been drafted with little or no consultation with Aboriginal people.*

More recently framed legislation, however, has acknowledged that not only do Koories have an enduring interest in their own heritage, but also have sufficient knowledge and experience in management of that heritage. In 2006 a new Act, which reflects these changes, was passed to afford protection for Koorie sites in Victoria. The *Aboriginal Heritage Act* 2006 (No. 16 of 2006) commenced from 28 May 2007, and replaced the Commonwealth *Aboriginal and Torres Strait Islander Heritage Protection Act* 1984, as well as the *Archaeological and Aboriginal Relics Preservation Act* 1972, which had been in operation since 1972.

Key features of the *Aboriginal Heritage Act* 2006 include the creation of the Aboriginal Heritage Council, which advises on the protection of Aboriginal heritage and comprises traditional owners; the use of cultural heritage management plans for certain development plans or activities; the ability for Registered Aboriginal Parties to evaluate management plans, advise on permit applications, enter into cultural heritage agreements and negotiate the repatriation of Aboriginal human remains. Under Section 24 of this Act, a person who discovers what he or she knows to be an Aboriginal place or object must report it to the Secretary of the Department of Planning and Community Development.

## Archaeological field work

Systematic regional field archaeology began in 1973 with the passing of the first legislation to protect Aboriginal sites. A small department called the Archaeological and Aboriginal Relics Preservation Office (AARPO) was set up to administer and carry out the functions of the Act. Originally located within the chief secretary's department, it was transferred to Ministry for Conservation in 1975. In the following year the AARPO was retitled the Victoria Archaeological Survey (VAS). In September 1983 VAS became part of the Ministry for Planning and Environment. From July 1993, protection of Koorie archaeological sites became the responsibility of Aboriginal Affairs Victoria and that part of VAS that looked after Koorie sites became the Aboriginal Heritage Services Branch of Aboriginal Affairs.

The basic aims of the Victoria Archaeological Survey was to record and protect Koorie archaeological sites, research the Koorie past of this state and educate the public about archaeology and the Koorie history of Victoria. Initially, most of the work done by VAS was in rural Victoria, particularly in the Western District and eastern Gippsland. In later years the department supervised three major studies around the Port Phillip region.

The archaeology department at La Trobe University has developed significantly since its beginnings in 1976. Field work by staff and students has been spread over most parts of the state and for some years there was a continuing excavation at a cave site in eastern Gippsland. Jim Allen was appointed as the department's foundation professor in 1985. What is now the archaeology program within the School of Humanities and Social Science has a staff of about fifteen members, with research interests that range widely in time and place.

## Archaeological studies

Excavation is one method archaeologists use to find out about the past, but it is only a very small part of the archaeologist's job. Excavation of an archaeological site is done for specific purposes and only after a careful weighing up of the possible benefits against the costs, and the costs in time and energy, are significant. To begin with, an archaeological excavation, of whatever size, is a complex and labour-intensive exercise that requires the input of significant material resources. But the actual digging is only the first step in the process of acquiring data; it needs to be followed up by time spent in analysing the material retrieved from the site. This stage can take as much as ten times as long as the digging. Following detailed analysis of the finds, the data then must be considered in its context and conclusions drawn in the final report.

Perhaps the most important question to consider before an archaeological site is excavated is whether the information expected to be gained by digging warrants destroying the site. What is taken out can never be put back. This indisputable fact means the archaeologist carrying out the excavation must make sure that the record created during the dig—of details such as what was found, precisely where it was (in three dimensions, and what its relationship was to other finds—is as complete as it can be. In this way future researchers will be able to re-assess the site and draw their own conclusions, secure in the knowledge that although the site no longer exists as much information as possible was gained through its deliberate destruction.

Archaeologists study past societies by looking at the material remains that do still exist; basically it is the study of what those societies have left behind. Some archaeologists are interested in non-literate societies, that is, those that left no written records; others are more interested in industrial history, shipwrecks or goldmining. In Australia most archaeologists (but by no means all) investigate Aboriginal culture from the pre-contact period. The major employers of archaeologists in this country are state government departments, museums and universities, but there are also many self-employed consultant archaeologists.

Archaeological studies generally fall into two categories. One group consists of 'public' archaeologists, who are employed by state governments, either in full-time positions or as private consultants employed on a contractual basis in relation to a particular project. These professionals are mainly concerned with identifying and recording the evidence of the Aboriginal past so that it can be protected against future dangers. In this context the archaeological record is seen as a resource that needs to be managed for the future. The second category consists of archaeologists who work within an academic environment. The professionals in this group are more often concerned with developing answers to particular questions.

The major difference between these two types of study, at the very earliest stages, is the sort of questions that are asked. For site management purposes, it is important to know the locations and condition of sites; an academic study is generally more all-embracing but might concentrate, say, on economic aspects of Koorie lifestyle. In both cases there is a limited amount of time available to gather the information. For this reason, studies tend to be set out in more or less standard ways that will maximise the information gathered.

The first step in an archaeological project of any kind is to collate the relevant information. The results of previous studies are considered, as well as a range of information about the physical environment and history of the area. This overview of previous work is necessary to provide a background to the study and a starting point for research. Consideration of historical sources that relate to Koories within the area of study may suggest that particular parts of the study area are more likely to contain archaeological evidence than others. It is at this stage, also, that the archaeologist can gain an understanding of the range of sites in the area, and of their regional significance.

## Historical evidence

The major non-archaeological sources of information about Koories are written documents. Although in pre-European times Koories made no written records, there is an immense body of information from the eighteenth century onwards compiled by European observers of their culture. Personal diaries, journals, field notes, and official reports and dispatches all of which emanate from the Aboriginal Protectorate are records sometimes referred to as 'ethno-historical sources' because they are historical documents that deal with a different ethnic group from that of the writer. While the observations these records contain are often of great value, the use of ethno-historical sources is often beset with problems. It must be remembered that statements made in private papers may be no more than the opinion of the writer, formed within his or her cultural milieu. Similarly, recorded observations can contain cultural biases or misconceptions on the part of the observer.

These biases colour the observer's record. Consider the disregard many Europeans had for Koorie religion. Devout Christians such as Wesleyan missionaries Francis Tuckfield and Joseph Orton considered that Koories were living without the benefit of God. Aboriginal religious form was particularly subtle; because they couldn't see the God of *their* religion, Tuckfield, Orton and others assumed Koorie culture was devoid of religious forms. As Orton wrote:

After the minutest observation and strictest inquiry I could not discover that they possess the most indistinct notion of a Supreme Being—nor have I been able to ascertain that they have the slightest vestige of religious worship or superstitious observance.

Koorie culture and the Koorie view of their connection to land were equally misunderstood by European settlers. Records of traditional Koorie life generally stress the ways in which the two cultures differ, and depict the Koories' way of life as inferior. The English colonists came from an agricultural society and their assessment of Koorie land use was based on their own experience. Many settlers had grown up in a world in which their culture was guided largely by the Bible. Thus they could cite the biblical injunction, in Genesis 1:28: 

> *Be fruitful, and multiply, and replenish the earth, and subdue it: and have dominion over the fish of the sea, and over the fowl of the air, and over every living thing that moveth upon the earth.*

This divine directive was taken to include the sowing of crops and animal husbandry. But Koories did none of these things, which suggested to many squatters that Koories weren't making proper use of the country. This type of ethno-centrism lay at the base of many of the negative observations made about the Koories in the Port Phillip region.

Of course the Europeans were not the only people with biases. Without doubt Koories would not have given Europeans access to information which they wished to protect, such as the location of sacred places or details of secret ceremonies. They may have responded to questions with answers that were false but intended to satisfy the questioner.

Ethno-historical sources must be used with care as they often raise as many questions as they answer. Despite this they also yield data that would not show up in the archaeological record. We might be able to tell from a study of the size of the campsites and organic remains that people travelled in groups and ate particular foods, but there is no visible trace in the archaeological record of how many people travelled together or who provided what types of food. Historical records reveal this type of information.

The same care needs to be exercised when using sources of information such as photographs, drawings and paintings. Elements that don't belong, but reflect how the artist sees the subject, are often included. Many early photographs of Koories supposedly in the bush were in fact taken in studios with canvas backdrops, and even outdoor shots were carefully posed according to Victorian notions of beauty or quaintness. It is fortunate nonetheless that the photographic process had been developed at the time of European settlement and that cameras were used from an early date, because many valuable photographs were taken of the landscape and its original inhabitants.

Documentary sources also often contain useful data about the past environment, such as descriptions of landscape, or of plants and animals that were once abundant but are now rare. The major problem with records such as explorers' field notes and diary accounts of trips into the bush is that we cannot be sure that the writer always knew what he was looking at. The observations were often made by people unfamiliar with the flora and fauna they saw. Plant species in particular were wrongly identified, or likened to similar but unrelated plants from the other side of the world.

## Other evidence

To learn about changes in the landscape, and flora and fauna in the distant past, the archaeologist draws on disciplines such as geology, geography, botany and zoology.

Geological processes, such as the building up and wearing away of river terraces, volcanic eruptions, erosion of ground surfaces and changes in sea level all leave evidence that presents a picture of a changing landscape. We know that at some period in the past the sea level has been higher because at Altona, for example, there is a bed of seashells about one metre above the present water level in the bay. There are also coastal areas where the ground surface is composed of marine silts and sand, deposited during periods when the area was under water. We know that in the past sea level has also been lower than today because when this happened there was a period of rapid stream bed erosion. The river alters the angle of its bed so that its speed, and the amount of waterborne silt, is the same as before. If we find an indication of rapid erosion in riverbeds it can be evidence of a lower sea level. Sometimes coral reefs are found at a greater depth underwater than the depths where they are forming today. This is another indication of the sea having been lower at some time in the past, because reefs will form only in specific circumstances.

Changes in climate, such as greater rainfall or higher average temperatures, can sometimes be shown through the study of microscopic seeds or pollen. Pollen is found in silts and sediments deposited over a long period of time. Botanists usually collect pollen in cores (cylindrically shaped cross-sections) from places like lake beds, but it has also been found in archaeological sites. Pollen of particular plants found in a situation of known date point to those plants having grown in the area at that time. Plants are often very sensitive to local climatic conditions, so if mosses and other species that like the cold are discovered, it is evidence that the climate then was colder and wetter.

## The site

The fundamental form of archaeological evidence is the material remains of a society, and to discover these the archaeologist has to get out into the field and survey the area. In most cases the study area is far larger than can be covered in the available time, so a sampling strategy is developed and a percentage of the area is investigated. Informed by the background data already acquired, the archaeologist chooses parts of the area which will be representative of the whole. This choice is often made on the basis of different types of environment within the study area, and the historical record of Koorie use of the area.

In conducting surveys, the archaeologist usually walks over an area, examining the ground surface in a straight line about ten metres wide. Large areas are transected by zigzag paths or crossed backwards and forwards at ten-metre intervals. Some types of Aboriginal site are more visible than others, but the less vegetation there is on the surface the better; for this reason, ploughed fields are especially favoured. Many hours of archaeological field work have been spent walking up and down market garden furrows. Discrete scatters of stone tools and waste flakes are generally easy to see and even isolated small flakes about one centimetre long can be spotted with practice.

During field work all discovered sites are recorded and plotted on base maps. At a later planning stage, judgments will be made of the likely existence of undiscovered sites. This assessment will be based on the number and type of site already recorded. With the sites recorded and plotted on maps it is easier to relocate them for protection or management. Maps of site locations are also valuable in reconstructing the lifestyle of the people who lived in the area.

## Interpretation

With the data gathered through field work and the earlier literature searches, the archaeologist is now ready for the most important part—the interpretation of the accumulated evidence. In essence the archaeologist writes a story, based on the evidence, which explains the patterns (or lack of them) we see in the material remains.

What we know about the prehistoric population of any area depends on the evidence we have; what clues are available to tell us about the past? Any book about the past is in large part a reconstruction of earlier events or ways of life. How true the reconstruction is depends on how complete the evidence is, and on the efficacy of the interpretation. The further away in time the researcher is, the more difficult it is to reconstruct the past, because there is less evidence and it is harder to understand. Interpretation becomes much harder, too, when the researcher and the subject belong to different racial groups. As noted above, Koories are increasingly researching their own past and becoming directly involved in archaeology.

When archaeologists interpret their evidence they use models, which may be based on analogies drawn from anthropological studies of contemporary or recent societies, thought to be analogous to the subject past society. Analogies of this kind might relate to a wide range of aspects of society, as simple as how humans dispose of their rubbish or as complex as ecological relationships between groups and their environment.

Whatever the purpose of an archaeological study, the result is an increase in the amount of information we have about the pre-contact past. As part of a study, new sites are recorded which may provide additional data about how Koories lived before the European invasion. The study may be all that is known of the prehistoric Koories of that area, and will serve as the starting point for another, future study which will in turn again increase our knowledge of the subject. 

## Dating a site

Without some means of determining how old a site is, archaeologists could not say whether it was older or younger than other sites in the area, or how long it had been since the site or object was made or used. This would make it impossible to talk meaningfully about cultural change, or to relate a site to changes in environmental factors.

There are two types of dates used by archaeologists when referring to the age of a site, differentiated on the basis of whether a relative date or an absolute date is given. With relative dating, a site is said to be older or younger, *relative to* another site or natural feature, for which an absolute date is known. With absolute dating something is taken from the site and subjected to a scientific process, from which an absolute figure can be calculated. The most widely used technique for deriving an absolute date is the radiocarbon process.

## Relative dating

In relative dating an estimate is arrived at in relation to other sites or other artefacts at the same site. Such estimates usually involve a reference point, such as an artefact type or a geological layer, the date of which has been fixed in absolute terms. In Australia it is known that a particular range of small tools called microliths do not appear in Aboriginal sites that have been dated by the radiocarbon method to before about 5000 years ago. So when these sorts of tools are found in a site, we can say that the site is no older than about 5000 years. Almost all campsites containing stone tools in the land of the Eastern Kulin have microliths so it is clear that Koories were camping all through this area within the past 5000 years.

In some cases, where many sites exhibiting stratified layering have been investigated, it might be possible to describe a sequence of artefacts—that Type A always appears in the sequence earlier than Type B. So if a new site is discovered that contains only Type B artefacts, although we cannot say how old it is, it can immediately be seen to be younger than any other site that contains Type A artefacts.

Within a site itself there is a good indication of the relative age of material. The basic principle for understanding the sequence of events which created an archaeological site is that the lowest layers are the earliest. If some charcoal is collected from the uppermost layer and radiocarbon dated to 2000 years BP (Before Present), everything from the levels below the charcoal layer must be older than 2000 years. How much older often cannot be said with any precision.

## Radiocarbon dating

Carbon-14 is a radioactive isotope of C-12 produced from nitrogen-14 in the atmosphere by cosmic radiation. It acts exactly like C-12, and is taken into all living matter. The proportions of the two forms of carbon are identical throughout the atmosphere and biosphere (the vegetable and animal kingdoms). When plants and animals die they cease to exchange their carbon, as carbon dioxide, with the atmosphere, and it is not replenished. The amount of C-14 (radiocarbon) dwindles by decay at a known rate (known as the half-rate). Because we know what that rate is, if we can discover the proportion of C-14 to C-12 in an archaeological sample, it becomes possible to calculate the age of the sample, or more accurately the time elapsed since the death of the living organism whose sample we have.

Since its invention in the 1940s by Willard Libby, the radiocarbon method has been further developed. Now, through the application of Accelerator Mass Spectrometry (AMS), the amount of material from which a date can be derived has been reduced from grams to milligrams, and even, in the right circumstances, micrograms. As well as this, AMS dating also has the potential to provide dates directly from objects and features of a site that previously were not possible, such as a tool, painting or bone.

Hitherto, all of these features could be dated by association only, but because such small quantities can now be used the technique can be applied to residues on stone tools, to organic materials in paint at art sites, and to bone. 

In using this dating method, three features of the scientific technique need to be allowed for: firstly, the 'date' given is never exact. The ± figure, which should always be quoted, is a statistical one, meaning that there is a two to one chance that the correct date lies within that bracket. For example, a date given as '2000 ± 300 years BP' means that there is a 66 per cent probability that the actual date of the sample lies between 1700 and 2300 years Before Present. (By convention, the 'present' is taken to be 1950.)

Secondly, it has been discovered that the half-life of radiocarbon (the time it takes for half the amount to decay) is longer than Libby originally calculated. The earliest dated samples were based on a half-life of 5568 ± 30 years. Later measurements of the Libby half-life indicated the figure was *about* 3 per cent too low and a more accurate half-life was 5730 ± 40 years. The dates obtained in early laboratory determinations need to be multiply by 1.03, to obtain the more accurate figure.

Thirdly, and more seriously, the assumption that the rate of production of C-14 has been uniform throughout past time is now challenged. The agreement between C-14 dates and historical dates or figures based on tree ring dating for the past 2000 years or so has been very close. For dates earlier than that, however, serious discrepancies have been found, suggesting that prior to about 2000 years ago the natural occurrence of C-14 was greater. This means that in this period true solar-year dates or samples are substantially earlier than the radiocarbon dates indicate. Over the past ten years radiocarbon dates have been made on timber from US bristlecone pine and German and Irish oak, for which there are firm sequences of dates, derived by dendrochronology. In this way a calibration curve has been produced that extends more than 10,000 years into the past and allows correction of the error in radiocarbon years.

In some contexts, the applicability of the radiocarbon dating process is limited by the fact that the C-14 decay from a sample of more than about 50,000 years age is virtually impossible to detect. In Australia this means that sites relating to the original colonisation of the continent need to be dated using a different technique for absolute dating.

Because the process is costly and takes time, radiocarbon dating is generally only done where there is some imperative for having a date or range of dates for a site. In many cases, particularly in open sites such as campsites, there is no suitable material in a context suitable for radiocarbon dating; in others, such as shell middens, there is abundant material.

Charcoal is the best material from which to get a radiocarbon date but anything that was once living such as wood, bone or shell can be used. What is needed is that the material provided to a dating laboratory has some relationship to cultural material within the site—charcoal from a fireplace or bone that has a close spatial relationship with human artefacts. That way, there is a greater certainty that the age of the sample is also the age of the cultural material. One of the first applications of radiocarbon dating in Australia was carried out to determine the age of a human cranium that was unearthed near Keilor in 1940. What was dated were charcoal and samples of wood; the former from a similar level to that at which the cranium was found. The derived date was about 14,500 BP, at that time, the earliest evidence of humans in Australia.

## Other absolute dating techniques

Radiocarbon dating is by far the most commonly used absolute dating technique but there are other methods that have been used in the Australian archaeology, including the luminescence techniques, thermoluminescence and the closely related optically stimulated luminescence. These methods of obtaining dates depend on an ability to measure the amount of energy trapped in minerals like quartz and feldspars when exposed to luminescence. Optical dating was invented in 1984 in the physics department at Simon Fraser University in Canada.

To simplify the process of luminescence dating, both thermoluminescence and optically stimulated luminescence rely on the fact that certain minerals (calcite, feldspar, and quartz) store energy derived from the sun—they do this at a known rate. This energy is lodged in the imperfect lattices of the mineral's crystals. Heating these crystals (such as when a pottery vessel is fired or when rocks are heated) empties the stored energy, after which time the mineral begins absorbing energy again.

Thermoluminescence dating compares the energy stored in a crystal to what would be expected to be there, thereby coming up with a date-of-last-heated. In similar fashion, optically stimulated luminescence dating measures the period elapsed since an object was last exposed to sunlight. One of the best known archaeological sites in Australia, the burial site of Australia's oldest human find, Mungo man, was dated in 2003 using optically stimulated luminescence.

Luminescence dating has an advantage over radiocarbon dating in that dates of between a few hundred years to several hundred thousand years can be achieved. This makes it more useful in an Australian context, where it is likely that early Aboriginal sites could be from 60,000 to 70,000 years old.

CHAPTER TEN

# Archaeological Site Types

Artefacts and sites that provide archaeologists with information about how Koories lived in pre-contact times have been found all over the land of the Eastern Kulin. Indeed, within this area more than 3,500 archaeological sites have been recorded to date.

It's important to note, however, that recorded archaeological sites and objects are not spread evenly through any given area. The occurrence of sites reflects the patterns of life of pre-contact Koories, which were largely determined by the seasonal availability of natural resources. Campsites and places of regular activity needed to be near a source of fresh water, so it is likely that most habitation sites will be recorded a short distance from a stream or other source of fresh water.

The number of sites recorded within a given area may often be a reflection of how much archaeological work has been done in that area—within the territories of the Woi wurrung and Boon wurrung, about 15 per cent of the recorded sites and objects are in the Westernport Bay/Mornington Peninsula area. This is a result of the detailed surveys that have been undertaken there,

The Corroboree tree in Richmond, photographed 1909. Whilst there is no necessary connection between trees and the location of corroborees, this one also appears to be scarred. As fewer and fewer old trees remained in the Melbourne area, it was assumed by some European residents that these remnants were associated with dances that had been witnessed in early settlement days.

more than anything else. A similar survey completed in Watha wurrung territory on the Bellarine Peninsula greatly increased the number of known sites in that area. Archaeological research is going on all the time, and in the course of surveys carried out for a range of purposes, as well as accidental discovery of sites or objects, the number of recorded sites is always increasing.

An archaeological site of the kind considered here is any location where evidence of pre-contact Koorie activity can be found. Although these sites can vary in their nature, size, frequency of occurrence and information they provide, they all have at least one feature in common—they are all places where some human activity has occurred. 'Activity' in this context encompasses the widest range of economic, cultural, artistic and ceremonial endeavour. Because of the variations in circumstances in which they were formed, sites vary both in nature and complexity; this variation takes in a range of possibilities, resulting in different site types. The types of sites that have been recorded within the land of the Eastern Kulin, in order of the frequency in which they occur, are: shell middens, campsites/open sites, scarred trees, isolated artefacts, quarries, grinding grooves, burials, rock wells, ceremonial sites, and art sites. Complex sites, such as shell middens and campsites, have more complex stories to tell than isolated artefacts, but all of these site types are valuable and constitute first-hand evidence for the Koorie way of life.

## Shell middens

More than 350 coastal shell middens have been recorded on the Morning and Bellarine peninsulas and Phillip Island, making this type of archaeological site the most common in the clan estates of the Boon wurrung. 'Midden' is a Danish word that means 'rubbish heap' and so much is clear when they are examined. The shellfish—mussels, limpets, turbos and scallops—were eaten and their shells discarded on a rubbish heap, often with other food refuse such as bones. These rubbish heaps marked the places near where Koorie groups camped; from the size of the heap of shells in some cases it seems only long enough to eat a meal, while other accumulations can extend over hundreds of metres in length and have very clearly separated stratified layers.

When people lived repeatedly on the same spot, layers of rubbish and material built up. If a substantial period has elapsed between visits, there may be a layer of sand or dirt between the layers of material left by people. When a site is studied in detail, each of these layers, both cultural and natural, is carefully dug through by the archaeologist until the bottom of the site is reached. By collecting and studying the excavated contents of each layer the archaeologist can build up a picture of the sequence of events at the site.

Middens typically occur close to the coast, often in the foredunes where the sandy surface makes for comfortable camping. At Sandringham and Brighton there are rare examples of middens within the Melbourne metropolitan area, indicative of many others that have been destroyed through urban development. Freshwater shell middens occur too, usually within the vicinity of permanent river and stream courses. One was recorded on the Merri Creek near Coburg during the 1930s.

The species of shellfish within these middens provide clues to the foraging strategies of the Koories who lived in the area. If the midden consists of a single species of shell, say a rock platform species, then it is clear that the Koories preferred that particular shellfish to others. Where other types are available, this sort of specialisation may have been for practical reasons—because they were easier to collect, or perhaps, they tasted better. The size of the shells in the midden gives an indication of what season they were caught, how much food they would have provided and how efficient the gathering strategies of the Koories would have been.

Larger middens are generally indicative of a major habitation site, so we might expect to find other archaeological remains in addition to shells. Large middens often contain the bones of scaled fish and terrestrial animals, and stone and bone tools.

## Surface campsites

These open sites may mark the spot of a lengthy stay in a base camp or be the result of a brief episode in the day-to-day life of pre-contact Koories. This type of site is typically identified from small pieces of stone exposed on the ground surface within a definable area. Although most campsites consist of nothing more than a scatter of stone artefacts, they sometimes contain other cultural remains such as hearth stones and bone. Organic remains are rarely found because they are destroyed more easily. It is the stone tools which survive, often as the only evidence of human activity in the area.

Small surface scatters of stone tools and waste flakes mark the places where men carried out maintenance on their toolkits, such as making new stone points for their spears, or making stone tools for scraping skins, cutting, or shaping wood. This activity might be done in camp, usually off to one side to avoid leaving sharp stone pieces around for people to step on, or in a location where the men waited for game. Within Victorian campsites, of every one hundred pieces of stone found about eighty-five are waste flakes. The rest are formally shaped tools, pieces of core material, or stones which show evidence of having been used for some purpose.

The material used to make these artefacts is a range of medium to fine-grained stone, including silcrete, chalcedony and chert. All of these materials have a component of silica, which serves to bind the grains in a homogeneous matrix. This is important because it facilitates flaking of the stone from a core nodule and a secondary retouch to make a specially shaped tool such as blades, points and scrapers. Outcroppings of silcrete, which was favoured for making such small flaked implements, are known to occur in the Keilor and Mornington Peninsula areas.

The size of recorded camp sites, as indicated by scatters of stone, varies widely, from a couple of metres across, to hundreds of metres. This type of site is usually found within a short distance of a fresh water source. In areas that are prone to flooding such sites are sometimes indicated by the occurrence of a low earthen mound. More than 2,300 surface campsites of all types have been recorded within the estates of the Eastern Kulin. Many such sites must have been destroyed in the past one hundred and seventy-five years.

Campsites are particularly subject to erosion and whatever material has been discarded will be dispersed, although such sites may have been used more than once, they rarely show any layering that would indicate different periods of occupation. Layering of this kind, or stratification, does occur in places of regular habitation that are protected from the elements, such as caves or rock shelters. 

## Scarred trees

Scarred trees are probably the most easily recognisable type of Koorie site. At least 700 examples have been recorded to date within the land of the Eastern Kulin, many as a result of information given by members of the public. The site consists of a tree—living or dead—from which a slab of bark has been removed for use in any number of ways. The removal of the bark, usually with a stone hatchet, does not kill the tree but creates a generally symmetrical scar which is clearly visible. The symmetry of the scar is one criterion used in assessing whether it was the result of human action, or a natural cause. Other considerations are that, by and large, the scar does not run to the ground, and that the tree is old enough to have been used by Koories in the pre-contact period. For this it would need to be at least 175 years of age.

Sometimes these sites are referred to as 'canoe trees' though not all of the bark used for canoes. Cutting bark for containers or slabs to make a shelter would have caused many of the scars we see today. The size of the scar is generally a guide to the use of the bark and can range in length from thirty to forty centimetres to as much as five metres. A well known tree in the Melbourne suburb of Doveton has a scar of about four and a half metres.

Trees which show scars created by making toeholds in order to climb the tree and catch possums are also included in this category of site. They are not as common as the usual scarred tree but there are a couple of examples of this type in the Geelong area.

Scarred trees are found often close to permanent streams. This may be because the most suitable trees grew near water, or simply because these trees haven't been cleared for building. There are a number surviving in the Yarra River valley in the Heidelberg and Eaglemont areas, which suggests that such sites were once more widespread. Eucalypts such as the River Red Gum (*Eucalyptus camaldulensis*) and Grey Box (*E. Macrocarpa*) were favoured for their bark.

## Isolated artefacts

As well as the small stone tools commonly found in Koorie surface campsites throughout this region, at many places larger stone tools such as stone hatchet heads, grinding stones (mortars and pestles) and hammer-stones have been recorded. These relics are usually found in isolation and are referred to and recorded as isolated finds. The information that can be gained from them is not great but it is of some interest and value to know where such artefacts have been located.

Many of these isolated finds are stone hatchet heads which were once fixed by gum and sinew, with the aid of a groove, to wooden handles. In an archaeological context the handle and binding does not often survive and the hatchet head alone is the usual find. Other large tools such as grinding stones (used in the preparation of food and for powdering ochre), pounders and hammer-stones have also been recorded. These artefacts are often discovered in areas where the native vegetation is substantially untouched and the ground surface has not been extensively disturbed. In areas where farming has been carried on since European settlement, it is not uncommon for local landowners to have collections of this type of artefact.

## Mount William axe trade

At Mount William near Lancefield, seventy-eight kilometres from Melbourne, there is a source of stone which was much prized for making stone hatchet heads. The stone is a volcanic material called diorite, which keeps a sharp edge once it is ground. The area surrounding the outcrops is covered with the debris of many years quarrying by Koories. The area covered by this site today is more than forty hectares.

Use of this stone for making hatchet heads was not restricted to the Woi wurrung territory, however, or the much larger area of the Eastern Kulin. Highly specialised studies of the stone's composition have allowed us to identify pieces of stone from the Mount William quarry wherever they are found. In this way hatchets have been traced to sites in New

South Wales and South Australia, up to 700 kilometres away from the source. These stone hatchet heads moved through a trading network that existed between friendly clans, and involved the exchange of particular commodities for pre-shaped but unground hatchet blanks. These pieces of stone were taken away in an unfinished state and later had an edge ground onto it. This was done by rubbing the blank against an abrasive agent, such as a sandstone outcrop, to form a sharp cutting edge. To make the handle, a length of wood was split at one end and the hatchet head inserted. The head was then bound with kangaroo sinew with resinous gum gathered from trees applied.

The quarry was still being used when European settlement began, and much of what we know about its operation and the exchange value of the stone is from European records of the time. Access to the stone was clearly defined and carefully controlled. The site was within the estate of the Gunung-willam-balluk and in the early 1840s the primary right to operate the quarry belonged to the Ngurungaeta of that clan, Ningulabul. He was assisted in this role by a number of other clan-heads including Billibellary of the Wurundjeri willam. They supervised the quarrying and distribution of the stone at Mount William. Infringement of the procedure for acquiring the stone was regarded as a serious breach of accepted protocol. Incidents did occur however, and there are reports of one such breach, by a young Watha wurrung man from the vicinity of Geelong a few years prior to European settlement. When the theft was discovered, Billibellary called a meeting to ascertain whether the man acted alone, or under direction from his clan-head. Finding the man had acted out of ignorance, Billibellary told the Watha wurrung elders to caution him not to repeat the offence.

A variety of commodities were exchanged for the Mount William stone. A possum-skin cloak could be exchanged for three hatchet blanks, which suggests a high value (in terms of work-hours) for the blanks. And a particular type of reed used as spear shafts was traded from the Swan Hill area. What was acquired from the custodian of the quarry were pieces of diorite that had been pre-shaped by flaking to the approximate size required for a hatchet head.

It is not known exactly how the pieces of stone were removed from the outcropping at the quarry. They may have been levered off using a stout stick, probably with a fire-hardened tip or a fire may have been lit at the base of the outcrop to heat the stone, which would have then been dowsed with water. The sudden cooling would cause the rock to fracture. There are also indications that less exposed outcropping were excavated to obtain the stone.

Most of the Mount William stone hatchets that have been found show very little wear, which suggests they were prized more as social objects than as practical ones. A hatchet which has been well used has to be resharpened. This process reduces the size of the head, eventually to the point where it is too small for use. This is not the case with most Mount William hatchets. They seem to have been passed on as valued exchange items which were treasured for themselves and not used.

By plotting the areas where the hatchets have been found, it is possible to gain some idea of the location of social boundaries in prehistoric Victoria. Hatchet heads might end up a great distance from their source as a result of being exchanged a number of times, but it is clear that the initial exchange was carried out between members of two friendly groups. We can see, then, that the area in which these hatchets are found coincides with that of groups that were allied in some way. Most Mount William hatchets have been found within or close to what was Kulin territory. The hatchets found in New South Wales and South Australia would have been exchanged from group to group. Conversely, there are only rare instances of Mount William hatchets in Gunai territory, in Gippsland, bearing out the belief that Kulin clans and those of the Gunai were hostile to each other.

Not all hatchet heads found within the area of the Eastern Kulin came from Mount William although that quarry was probably the most important in the region. There are other sources of suitable stone for grinding in Watha wurrung territory near Geelong, at Mount Camel, and also near Howqua, south of Mansfield.

## Grinding grooves

These sites are associated with the production of edge-ground hatchets.

When the edge is ground on a hatchet head, it is done against an abrasive surface. Boulders of sandstone outcroppings at ground surface were used for this purpose. The operation creates a groove in the grittier surface which becomes enlarged with repeated use. Because rocks suitable for grinding are uncommon, when a source was found it was frequently used, so many of these sites have a large number of grooves in their surface. Small pieces of abrasive sandstone were sometimes carried around as portable grinding grooves for use in temporary resharpenings. Five sites of this type have been recorded in Taung wurrung and Woi wurrung territory; perhaps the best known is near Mount Macedon, not far from the stone quarry at Mount William.

## Burials

This type of site is usually discovered accidentally, in many cases during mining or quarrying activities, though sometimes burials have been exposed by natural erosion. In most cases where human skeletons are uncovered, a salvage excavation is carried out to avoid destruction of the remains. It is current practice for Koorie skeletal material to be reburied in another locality.

As a type of site, burials can tell us something of the Koorie past. In some cases dates have been obtained from material in the burial. At Green Gully, close to the Maribyrnong River, a double burial was discovered in 1965. This was later dated by the radiocarbon method to about 6500 BP. A stone tool from the site and charcoal from a fire suggested that the site may be about 17,000 years old. The burials at Green Gully were interesting because the bones were later found to belong to two different individuals—a male and a female. It is clear that the bones had been buried long after the people had died and that the bodies had been left to dry out before being buried. Whether the 'double' burial was intended or an accident caused by two bodies being mixed at the time of interment is not known. As with other ceremonial activity, the mortuary practices of pre-contact Koories is not well known.

In 1977 a group of Koorie burials were discovered during sand mining close to the Werribee River. These burials were about 7,300 years old and, like the burial at Green Gully, the bodies of the individuals, two adults and a child, had been allowed to dry out before burial. One feature of these burials was that the bones had been stained with red ochre.

As well as giving us an idea of the age of Koorie occupation of the area, these burials tell us something about the culture of these Koories. Their burial practices suggest that they had a developed notion of the afterlife, and of the 'proper' way in which their dead went to join it.

## Rock wells

Rock wells are places where fresh water can be obtained, in areas where there is a dearth of freshwater streams. They are natural landscape features, such as an interior cavity in a large boulder or rock outcrop, where rainwater collects. In some cases Koories may have modified the rock surface to allow water to more easily flow into the cavity. In the mountain ranges of the You Yangs, four rock wells in the shape of natural depressions in the granite rock surface have been recorded. These wells are around 40 to 70 cm deep and show no sign of modification by Koories. In some areas the natural water table is high and a different type of well taps into underground water sources. After any debris is cleared from the well, water percolates into the bottom out of the aquifer. Two rock wells have been recorded within Tuang wurrung estates. A well of this kind is located at Beaumaris in Boon wurrung territory.

## Ceremonial sites

These are among the rarest of sites in Aboriginal archaeology. There are fewer of them by virtue of their nature and are generally hard to access. They are also rare because they are not always recognised, which has led to their destruction on many occasions. These sites often consist of an arrangement of rocks on the surface, in a particular shape or pattern. There are instances of such rocks being moved during farming activities, such as the building of fences, grazing of stock or ploughing. In some cases these rock arrangements may be associated with a ditch or a bank, usually circular in shape.

There are five sites recorded in the Port Phillip region which may be of ceremonial significance. Four of these sites are in the vicinity of Sunbury and the fifth is near Mount Rothwell, to the west of Geelong. The Sunbury sites consist of circular ditches with an associated cairn of stones in the centre. The Mount Rothwell stone arrangement, called Wurdi Youang, is one of only four recorded stone arrangements in Victoria. It is a roughly egg-shaped arrangement of stones set into the surface of the ground.

Ceremonial sites are the most difficult for archaeologists to interpret because they relate to a part of traditional Koorie life that left little in the way of material remains. Moreover, there are very few accounts, and none wholly accurate, of the sorts of activities that were carried on at these sites. Thus, if ceremonies took place at these sites, it is a matter of conjecture today as to the nature of those ceremonies, what their meaning was and who the participants were.

## Art sites

The occurrence of art sites is largely dependent on the availability of suitable surfaces to be able to create art as well as requiring some natural protection from the elements. Victoria is not rich in such sites and only four have been recorded in the land of the Eastern Kulin. These are south-east of Euroa and on the northern side of the Great Dividing Range. A wide range of motifs have been painted on granite surfaces in red and include human figures, dogs, tracks of kangaroo and emu. There is no historical evidence of the function or use of these sites but it should be said, however, that a lack of art sites cannot be taken as a lack of artistic expression on the part of the Eastern Kulin. What it means is that this expression took different forms including body decoration, designs on shields, boomerangs, the underside of possum-skin cloaks and in personal adornments.

## Conclusion

Our understanding of the lives of Eastern Kulin before contact with Europeans is largely based on the interpretation of recorded archaeological sites of the types described here. Study of these material remains provides clues and insights into their way of life but there is much that cannot be seen. This situation may improve through time, as more sites are recorded and new interpretations developed, but our knowledge will always be limited accordingly. While historical evidence offers some help in recreating the lost patterns of Eastern Kulin life, it also has limitations. Even first-hand observations must be read with caution, allowing for cultural biases and a lack of knowledge. Further, our understanding of the Eastern Kulin in the pre-contact past is hampered by a lack of empathy. As anthropologist Diane Barwick wrote:

> *No living person can fully understand the sentiments of people who lived a century ago.*

Despite the limitations of archaeological and historical sources, and the distance in time between us, what we know about the Eastern Kulin suggests their way of life was both complex and sustainable. Although Koorie society is often referred to as 'traditional' it had sufficient flexibility to cope with environmental change, allowing the spiritual relationship between people and land to be the fundamental characteristic of their world.

# Sources

CHAPTER ONE THE KULIN LANDSCAPE


Beardsell, D. & Beardsell, C. (1999) *The Yarra: A natural treasure* (Melbourne: Royal Society of Victoria).

Calder, M. & Calder, W. (2002) *Victoria's Box-Ironbark country: a field guide* (Melbourne: Victoria National Parks Association).

Gill, E. D. (c. 1967) *Melbourne before history began* (ABC Books: Sydney).

Hall, T. S. (1909) Victorian hill and dale: A series of geological rambles (Melbourne: Thomas C. Lothian).

Hills, E. S. (1959) The physiography of Victoria: an introduction to geomorphology (Melbourne: Whitcombe & Tombs).

Marsden, M. (1973) Palaeozoic evolution of east-central Victoria' in McAndrew, J. & Marsden, M. (eds) *Regional Guide to Victorian geology.* (Second Edition) (Melbourne: University of Melbourne), pp. 175–201.

Otto, K. (2005) *Yarra: a diverting history of Melbourne's murky river* (Text Publishing: Melbourne).

Presland, G. (2008) *The place for a village: how nature has shaped the city of Melbourne* (Melbourne: Museum Victoria).

Pritchard, G.B., (1910) *The geology of Melbourne; as told by a few rambles in and around the city.* (Melbourne: Peter G. Tait).

Singleton, O.P. (1973) 'Mesozoic and Tertiary stratigraphy of the Otway Region' in McAndrew, J. & Marsden, M. (eds) *Regional Guide to Victorian geology.* (Second Edition) (Melbourne: University of Melbourne), pp. 114–128.

Spencer-Jones, D. (1973) 'Geology of the Geelong district' in McAndrew, J. & Marsden, M. (eds) *Regional Guide to Victorian geology.* (Second Edition) (Melbourne: University of Melbourne).

Thomas, D. E., (ed) (1967) *Bulletin No. 59 Geology of the Melbourne district, Victoria.* (Geological Survey of Victoria: Melbourne).

Vandenberg, A. H. M. (1973) 'Geology of the Melbourne district' in McAndrew, J. & Marsden, M. (eds) *Regional Guide to Victorian geology.* (Second Edition) (Melbourne: University of Melbourne), pp. 14–30.

## CHAPTER TWO THE PEOPLE

Barwick, D. E. (1985) 'Mapping the past: an atlas of Victorian clans 1835–1904' *Aboriginal History* 8: 100–130.

Blake, B. J. (1991) 'Woiwurrung, the Melbourne Language' in Dixon, R. M. W. & Blake, B. J. (eds) *Handbook of Australian Language: Volume 4, The Aboriginal Language of Melbourne and other grammatical sketches* (Melbourne: Oxford University Press) pp. 31–124.

Blake, B. J. & Reid, J. (1995) 'Classifying Victorian Languages' *La Trobe Papers in linguistics* 8: 1–55.

Campbell, A. H. (1988) *John Batman and the Aborigines* (Malmsbury: Kibble Books).

Clark, I. D. (1990) Aboriginal languages and clans: an historical atlas of western and central Victoria, 1800–1900 (Melbourne: Monash Publications in Geography 37).

Clark, I. D. (2001) *The Yalukit-willam, the first people of the City of Hobsons Bay* (Altona: City of Hobsons Bay).

Ellender, I. & Christiansen, P. (2001) *People of the Merri: the Wurundjeri in colonial days* (Merri Creek Management Committee).

Gaughwin, D. & Sullivan, H. (1984) 'Aboriginal boundaries and movements in Western Port, Victoria.' *Aboriginal History* 8: 80–98.

Gott, B. (2005) 'Aboriginal fire management in south-eastern Australia: aims and frequency' *Journal of biogeography* 32: 1203–1208.

Howitt, A. W. (1904) *The Native Tribes of south-east Australia* (London: MacMillan).

Morgan, J. (1967) *Life and adventures of William Buckley* (Melbourne: Heinemann).

Presland, G. (1998) *First residents of Melbourne's Western region* (Forest Hill: Harriland Press).

Presland, G. (2001) 'From the Birr-arrung to Willam-meering (Yarra River to Mount William): A journey through Aboriginal Victoria.' in Rasmussen, C. *et al. A Museum for the people* (Melbourne: Scribe).

Presland, G. (2002) 'People, land, spirit: Koorie life on the Yarra Yarra' *Victorian Historical Journal* 73: 21–33.

Presland, G. (2003) 'The landscape of the Wurundjeri' in *Rural remnants: some early Melbourne landscapes and what happened to them* (Melbourne: Yarra-Melbourne Local History Forum).

Smyth, R. B. (1878) *The Aborigines of Victoria and other parts of Australia* (Melbourne: John Ferris, Government Printer).

Stanner, W. E. H. (1979) 'Religion, totemism and symbolism' in *White man got no dreaming: Essays 1938–1973* (Canberra: Australian National University Press).

Stanner, W. E. H. (1987) 'The Dreaming' in Edwards, W. H. (ed) *Traditional Aboriginal society* Second Edition (Melbourne: Macmillan), pp. 227–238.

Stanner, W. E. H. (1998) 'Some aspects of Aboriginal religion' in Charlesworth, M. *Religious business*, (Melbourne: Cambridge University Press, 1998).

Thomas, W. notebook, manuscript collection, LaTrobe Library, Melbourne.

Thomas, W. private papers, uncatalogued manuscript collection, Mitchell Library, State Library of New South Wales, Sydney.

Thomson. D. F. (1949) Economic structure and the ceremonial exchange cycle in Arnhem Land (Melbourne: Macmillan).

Tindale, N. B. (1974) *Aboriginal tribes of Australia* (Canberra: Australian National University Press).

## CHAPTER THREE INTERCONNECTIONS IN THE KULIN WORLD

Barwick, D. E. (1985) 'Mapping the past: an atlas of Victorian clans 1835–1904' *Aboriginal History*, 8: 100–130.

Clark, I. D. (1990) Aboriginal languages and clans: an historical atlas of western and central Victoria, 1800–1900 (Melbourne: Monash Publications in Geography No. 37).

Hiatt, L. R. & Jones, R.M. (1990) 'Aboriginal conceptions of the workings of nature' in Home, R. W. (ed) *Australian science in the making* (Melbourne: Cambridge University Press/Australian Academy of Science), pp. 1–22.

Jones, R. M. (1990) 'Landscapes of the mind: Aboriginal perceptions of the environment' in Mulvaney, D. J. (ed) *The humanities and the Australian environment* (Canberra: Australian Academy of the Humanities, Occasional paper 11), pp. 21–48.

Sullivan, H. (1981) 'An archaeological survey of the Mornington Peninsula, Victoria' *Victoria Archaeological Survey Occasional Report Series* 6.

## CHAPTER FOUR LIFE ON THE EDGE OF THE BAY

Hiatt, B. (1978) 'Woman the gatherer' in Gale, F. (ed) *Woman's role in Aboriginal society* Third Edition (Canberra: Australian Institute of Aboriginal Studies), pp. 4–15.

Lee, R. B. (1968) 'What hunters do for a living, or, How to make out on scarce resources' in Lee R. B. & DeVore, I. (eds) *Man the hunter* (Chicago: Aldine), pp. 30–48.

Rose, F. G. G. (1987) The traditional mode of production of the Australian Aborigines (North Ryde: Angus & Robertson).

Sahlins, M. (1974) 'The original affluent society' in Sahlins, M. *Stone Age Economics* (London: Tavistock Publications), pp. 1–39.

Zola, N. & Gott, B. (1996) *Koorie Plants Koorie people* (Melbourne: Koorie Heritage Trust).

## CHAPTER FIVE A LARGE CAMP AT THE BOLIN WETLANDS

Frankel, D. (1982) 'An account of Aboriginal use of the Yam-daisy' *The Artefact* 7: 43–45.

Gibbins, H. (2010) 'Possum Skin Cloaks: tradition, continuity and change' in Russell, L. & Arnold, J. (eds) *Indigenous Victorians: repressed resourceful and respected. La Trobe Journal* 85: 125–140.

Gott, B. (1983) 'Murnong – *Microseris scapigera:* a study of a staple food of Victorian Aborigines' *Australian Aboriginal Studies* 2: 2–18.

Gott, B. (2005) 'Aboriginal fire management in south-eastern Australia: aims and frequency' *Journal of biogeography* 32: 1203–1208.

Jones, D., Mackay, S. & Pisani, A. (1997) 'Patterns in the Valley of the Christmas Bush: a seasonal

calendar for the upper Yarra Valley' *The Victorian Naturalist* 114: 246–249.
Kohen, J. L. (1995) *Aboriginal environmental impacts* (Sydney: University of New South Wales Press).

## CHAPTER SIX THE IMPACT OF WHITE SETTLEMENT

Barwick, D. E. (1971) 'Changes in the Aboriginal population of Victoria 1863–1966' in Mulvaney, D. J. & Golson, J. (eds) *Aboriginal man and environment in Australia* (Canberra: ANU Press), pp. 288–315.
Boys, R. D. (1959) First years at Port Phillip 1834–1842 preceded by a summary of historical events from 1768 (Melbourne: Robertson & Mullens).
Bride, T. F. (1983) (ed) *Letters from Victorian Pioneers* (Melbourne: Currey O'Neill).
Broome, R. (2005) *Aboriginal Victorians: a history since 1800* (Crows Nest: Allen & Unwin).
Butlin, N. G. (1983) Our original aggression: Aboriginal populations of southeast Australia 1788–1850 (Sydney: George Allen & Unwin).
Clark, I. D. (1995) *Scars in the landscape: a register of massacre sites in Western Victoria 1803–1859* (Canberra: Aboriginal Studies Press).
Clark, I. D. (2005) 'You have all this place, no good have children...' Derrimut: traitor, saviour, or a man of his people?' *Journal Royal Australian Historical Society* 91: 107–132.
Flemming, J. (1879) 'A journal of the explorations of Charles Grimes, Acting Surveyor-General of New South Wales' in Shillinglaw, J. J. (ed) *Historical Records of Port Phillip* (Melbourne: Victorian Government).
Tuckey, J. H. (1805) *An account of a voyage to establish a colony at Port Phillip in Bass's Strait on the south coast of New South Wales, in His Majesty's ship Calcutta, in the years 1802–3–4.* (London: Longman, Hurst, Rees and Orme).

## CHAPTER SEVEN THE PORT PHILLIP ABORIGINAL PROTECTORATE

Cannon, M. (ed) (1983) *Historical Records of Victoria*, Vols 2A and 2B. (Melbourne: Government Printer).
Cannon, M. (1993) *Black land, white land* (Melbourne: Minerva).
Christie, M. (1979) *Aborigines in colonial Victoria 1835–1886* (Sydney: Sydney University Press).
Clark, I. D. (1999) (ed) *Journals of G.A. Robinson, 1839–1849* (Melbourne: Heritage Matters).
Clark, I. D. (2010) 'George Augustus Robinson on Charles Joseph La Trobe: personal insights into a problematical relationship' in Russell, L. & Arnold, J. (eds) *Indigenous Victorians: repressed resourceful and respected. La Trobe Journal* 85: 13–21.
Clark, I. D. & Heydon, T. (2004) A bend in the Yarra: a history of the Merri Creek Protectorate Station and Merri Creek Aboriginal School 1841–1851 (Canberra: Aboriginal Studies Press).
Fels, M. H. & Rhodes, D. (1990) 'The Dandenong police paddocks' (3 vols) *Victoria Archaeological Survey Occasional Report Series* 25.
Presland, G. (1989) 'The journals of George Augustus Robinson' *La Trobe Library Journal* 11: 9–12.
Rhodes, D. (1995) 'An historical and archaeological investigation of the Loddon Aboriginal Protectorate station and Mount Franklin Aboriginal reserve' *Victoria Archaeological Survey Occasional Report Series* 46.

Attwood, B. (1989) *The making of the Aborigines* (Sydney: Allen & Unwin).
Attwood, B. (2008) *Possession: Batman's Treaty and the Matter of History* (Melbourne: Miegunyah).
Barwick, D. E. (1978) 'And the lubras are ladies now' in Gale, F. (ed) *Woman's role in Aboriginal society* Third Edition (Canberra: Australian Institute of Aboriginal Studies). pp. 51–63.
Barwick, D. E. (1998) *Rebellion at Coranderrk* (Canberra: Aboriginal History Monograph 5).
Broome, R. (2005) *Aboriginal Victorians: a history since 1800* (Crows Nest: Allen & Unwin).
Caldere, D. B. & Goff, D. J. (1991) *Aboriginal reserves and missions in Victoria* (Melbourne: Dept of Conservation and Environment).
Cato, N. (1976) *Mister Maloga* (St Lucia: University of Queensland Press).
Critchett, J. (1980) *Our land till we die: a history of Framlingham Aborigines* (Warrnambool: Warrnambool Institute Press).
Kenny, R. (2007) *The lamb enters the dreaming: Nathaneal Pepper & the ruptured world* (Melbourne: Scribe).
Massola, A. (1970) *Aboriginal missions stations in Victoria* (Melbourne: The Hawthorn Press).
Tonkin, D. & Landon, C. (1999) *Jackson's Track* (Melbourne: Viking).

## CHAPTER NINE INVESTIGATING THE PAST

Bowler, J. M., Johnston, H., Olley, J.M., Prescott, J.R., Roberts, R.G., Shawcross, W. & Spooner, N. A. (2003) 'New ages for human occupation and climatic change at Lake Mungo, Australia' *Nature* 421: 837–840.
Flood, J. (1995) *Archaeology of the dreamtime: the story of prehistoric Australia and its people* (Pymble, NSW: Angus & Robertson).
Frankel, D. (1991) *Remains to be seen: archaeological insights into Australian prehistory* (Melbourne: Longman Cheshire).
Griffiths, T. (1996) *Hunters and collectors: the antiquarian imagination in Australia* (Melbourne: Cambridge University Press).
Hale, H. & Tindale, N. (1930) 'Notes on some human remains in the Lower Murray valley, South Australia' *Records of the South Australia Museum* 4: 145–218.
Horton, D. (1991) *Recovering the tracks: the story of Australian archaeology* (Canberra: Aboriginal Studies Press).
Loy, T. (1993) 'On the dating of prehistoric organic residues' *The Artefact* 16: 46–49.
McCarthy, F. (1948) 'The Lapstone Creek excavation: Two culture periods revealed in eastern New South Wales' *Records of the Australian Museum* 22: 1–34.
Michaels, J. (1973) *Dating methods in archaeology* (New York: Seminar Press).
Mulvaney, D. J. & Kamminga, J. (1999) *Prehistory of Australia* (St Leonards, NSW: Allen & Unwin).
Murray, T. (ed) (1998) *Archaeology of Aboriginal Australia: a reader* (St Leonards, NSW: Allen & Unwin).
Presland, G. (1986) 'One hundred and fifty years of Aboriginal studies in Victoria' *The Artefact* 11: 13–28.
Presland, G. (2000) Scratching the surface: a brief history of the Victoria Archaeological Survey 1972–1994. [Unpublished souvenir booklet, prepared for re-union of VAS staff].

Roberts, R. & Jones, R. (1994) 'Luminescence dating of sediments: new light on the human colonisation of Australia' *Australian Aboriginal Studies* 2: 2–17.

Young , W. (2003) 'Mungo Man has his say on Australia's first humans' *New Scientist* 177 (2383): 15.

### CHAPTER TEN ARCHAEOLOGICAL SITE TYPES

Connah, G. (ed) (1983) *Australian field archaeology: a guide to techniques* (Canberra: Aboriginal Studies Press).

Coutts, P. J. F. & Miller, R. (1977) *The Mt William Archaeological Area* (Melbourne: Ministry for Conservation).

du Cros, H. (1989) *The western region: Melbourne metropolitan area: an archaeological survey.* (Melbourne: Victoria Archaeological Survey & The Western Region Commission).

Ellender, I. (1991) 'The city of Doncaster and Templestowe: the archaeological survey of Aboriginal sites' *Victoria Archaeological Survey Occasional Report Series* 43.

Gallus, A. S. (1971) Excavations at Keilor. Report No. 1. *The Artefact*, 27: 9–19.

Gaughwin, D. (1981) 'Sites of archaeological significance in the Westernport catchment' (Melbourne: Ministry for Conservation).

Gill, E. D. (1970) 'Antiquity and changing environment of the Australian Aborigines' in Pilling, A. & Waterman, R. (eds) *Diprotodon to detribalizaztion: studies of change among Australian Aborigines* (East Lansing: Michigan State University Press).

Gunn, R. G. (1981) 'The prehistoric rock art sites of Victoria: a catalogue' *Victoria Archaeological Survey Occasional Report Series* 5.

Gunn, R. G. (1992) 'The Ngurai-Illam Wurrung rock well at Whroo' *Victoria Archaeological Survey Occasional Report Series* 32.

Howitt, A. W. (1904) *The Native Tribes of south-east Australia* (London: MacMillan).

McBryde, I. (1984) 'Kulin greenstone quarries: the social contexts of production and distribution for the Mt William site' *World Archaeology* 16: 267–285.

McBryde, I. (1985) 'Exchange in south eastern Australia: an ethnohistorical perspective' *Aboriginal History*, 8: 132–153.

McCarthy, F. D. (1976) *Australian Aboriginal stone implements* (Sydney: The Australian Museum Trust).

Mitchell, S. R. (1949) *Stone Age Craftsmen* (Melbourne: Tait Publishing Co.).

Presland, G. (2001) 'From the Birr-arrung to Willam-meering (Yarra River to Mount William): a journey through Aboriginal Victoria' in Rasmussen, C. *et al. A Museum for the people.* (Melbourne: Scribe).

Rhoads, J. (1986) 'Bellarine peninsula: archaeological site assessment and management study' Unpublished report held at Aboriginal Affairs, Victoria.

Richards, T. & Jordan, J. (1999) 'Aboriginal archaeological investigations in the Barwon Drainage Basin' *Victoria Archaeological Survey Occasional Report Series* 50.

Sullivan, H. (1981) 'An archaeological survey of the Mornington Peninsula, Victoria' *Victoria Archaeological Survey Occasional Report Series* 6.

Waarden, N. Van (1986) 'An archaeological survey of the You Yangs' *Victoria Archaeological Survey Occasional Report Series* 23.

# Picture Credits

COVER
View of Aboriginal men with ceremonial marking on their bodies. Photograph by George W Priston. Pictures Collection. State Library of Victoria.

PAGE PRELIM XIII
Native encampment on the banks of the Yarra, c.1845. Watercolour by John Cotton. Pictures Collection. State Library of Victoria.

PAGE 6
Carrum Swamp, 2005. Digital artwork by Virginia Johnson. From the author's collection.

PAGE 10
Billibellary. Pencil drawing on card by William Thomas. Brough Smyth Papers, State Library of Victoria.

PAGE 13
Mr King, chief of the Gulburne tribe. Photograph by Carl Walter. Pictures Collection. State Library of Victoria.

PAGE 14
Map showing Eastern Kulin language area and clans. Reproduced from Aboriginal languages and clans by Ian D Clark.

PAGE 17
Map showing Watha wurrung language area and clans. Reproduced from Aboriginal languages and clans by Ian D Clark.

PAGE 19
Nerenunnin throwing a tirrer with a wongim in his left hand. Pen and pencil sketch by William Thomas. Brough Smyth Papers, State Library of Victoria.

PAGE 23
William Buckley, 1886. Etching reproduced in Picturesque Atlas of Australasia from sketch by W. MacLeod. State Library of Victoria.

PAGE 30
Aboriginal ceremony with emu and wallaby. Ochre painting on cardboard by William Barak. Pictures Collection. State Library of Victoria.

PAGE 32
Map of Port Phillip area by William Thomas. Source Gary Presland.

PAGE 35
William Barak, aged 33. Photograph by Carl Walter. Pictures Collection. State Library of Victoria.

PAGE 36
Lubras tattood to shew they have borne children, 1858. Photograph by A Fauchery/ R Daintree. Pictures Collection. State Library of Victoria.

PAGE 38
Native fight. Albumen silver photograph by D Le Souef. Pictures Collection. State Library of Victoria.

PAGE 43
Oil painting by Thomas Napier, c.1840. Royal Historical Society of Victoria. State Library of New South Wales.

PAGE 45
State Library of New South Wales/Artist S T Gill.

PAGE 48
Aboriginal Australian group camped in bush, 1933. Postcard. Pictures Collection. State Library of Victoria.

PAGE 50
Native encampment. Lithograph by J S Prout. Pictures Collection. State Library of Victoria.

PAGE 52
Melbourne from the falls, 1837. Hand coloured engraving by E L Montefiore. Pictures Collection. State Library of Victoria.

PAGE 56
Natives catching crayfish, c.1865. Wood engraving from a sketch by W A Cawthorne. Pictures Collection. State Library of Victoria

PAGE 58
Natives of Port Phillip, 1849. Tinted lithograph by H S Melville. Pictures Collection. State Library of Victoria.

PAGE 64
Merry Creek, (Plenty Ranges) 1864. Hand coloured lithograph. Artist unknown. Art Gallery of Ballarat.

PAGE 66
Rock well, Ricketts Point 1982. Photograph by Gary Presland.

PAGE 69
Native bathing scene on the Yarra Yarra river, 1847. Pen, ink and wash drawing on beige paper by John Cotton. Pictures Collection. State Library of Victoria.

PAGE 70
Emu sneaking. Hand coloured engraving by S T Gill. Mitchell Library, State Library of New South Wales.

PAGE 73
Drawing of Yam Daisy or Murnong by Beth Gott. Source Gary Presland.

PAGE 75
Australian Aboriginal group. Painting by G Mützel. Reproduced in F Ratzel, The History of mankind, 1896.

PAGE 76
Too Kings/Melbourne tribes when blacks first saw ship, c. 1865. Pen and ink drawing by Tommy McCrae. Pictures Collection. State Library of Victoria.

PAGE 81
Batman's treaty with the aborigines at Merri Creek, 6th June 1835. Oil on canvas by John Wesley Burtt, 1875. Pictures Collection. State Library of Victoria.

PAGE 86
Corroboree of Victorian natives. Silver gelatin photographic print by D Le Souef. Pictures Collection. State Library of Victoria.

PAGE 89
WT–AP, 1842 pencil sketch of William Thomas by George H Haydon. Brough Smyth Papers, State Library of Victoria.

PAGE 93
Chief Derah Mat [Derrimut] of Port Philip, 5 October 1836. Oil on canvas by Benjamin Duterrau. Dixson Galleries, State Library of New South Wales.

PAGE 94
George Augustus Robinson. Oil on canvas by Bernardino Giani (?), 1865. Mitchell Library, State Library of New South Wales.

PAGE 103

Windberry. Pencil drawing on card by William Thomas. Brough Smyth Paper. State Library of Victoria.

PAGE 106

Simon Wonga, aged 37, Chief of the Yarra Yarra, 1866. Photograph by Carl Walter. Pictures Collection. State Library of Victoria.

PAGE 108

Aboriginal men playing cricket in a paddock, 1904. Photograph by N Caire. Pictures Collection. State Library of Victoria.

PAGE 111

General view of Aboriginal Mission Station, Coranderrk, 1880. Photograph by Fred Kruger. Pictures Collection. State Library of Victoria.

PAGE 115

Victorian Aboriginals and canoe, 1880. Photograph by Fred Kruger. Pictures Collection. State Library of Victoria.

PAGE 116

Nov 1st /43 Loubras, 1843. Watercolour by Henry Godfrey. Pictures Collection. State Library of Victoria.

PAGE 136

Richmond Corroboree tree. Photograph, 1909. Photographer unknown. Royal Historical Society of Victoria.

# Index

## B



## C

## G



## H



## I



## J



## K



## L

P



R



S



T

## X



## Y